APPLE And Watch SE User Guide

The complete Beginners to Experts Users guide to mastering the iWatch Series 6 and Watch OS 7, with Illustrations, Hidden Features, Tips & Tricks, and Troubleshooting Common Problems.

NEWEL

GOMAN

Copyright

All rights reserved. No part of this publication The Apple Watch 6 and Watch SE User Guide may be reproduced, stored in a retrieval system or transmitted in any form or by any means, electronic, mechanical, photocopying, recording, scanning without permission in writing by the author.

Printed in the United States of America
© 2020 by NEWEL GOMAN

Churchgate Publishing House

USA | UK | Canada

Table of Contents

Copyright 2

CHAPTER ONE: GETTING READY FOR THE WATCH EXPERIENCE 15

WHAT IS NEW IN APPLE WATCH 6 AND THE APPLE WATCH SE? 15

How to set up and pair your Apple Watch with iPhone 19

How to turn on, pair, and set up your Apple Watch 19

How to set up Apple Watch using VoiceOver 22

Using Apple Watch 6 with cellular 24

How to activate/Add Apple Watch to your cellular plan 24

How to turn on/off cellular service on Apple Watch 25

How to check the data usage used by your Watch 25

How to remove your cellular plan 25

Are you having trouble pairing your Watch? 27

Are you seeing a Watch Face during pairing even when you are not sure whether you have paired your Watch with another iPhone before? 27

How to erase Apple Watch and settings 28

Your Camera cannot initiate the pairing? 29

If your Apple Watch is not pairing with iPhone 29

Make a move to connect your Apple Watch and iPhone again 30

Unpair your devices, then pair them again 31

How to unpair Apple Watch 31

How to pair more than one Apple Watch 31

How to quickly switch to a different Apple Watch 32

How to pair Apple Watch to a new iPhone 33

How to transfer an existing cellular plan to a new Apple Watch 34

How to charge Apple Watch 34

Check the time you last charge your Apple Watch 35

How to know your Watch's battery health 36

How to Lock or unlock Apple Watch 37

How to unlock Apple Watch 37

How to change passcode on the Apple Watch 39

How to disable Passcode if you don't want to use it to unlock your Watch. 40

How to lock Watch automatically 40

How to lock your Watch manually 41

What to do when you forget your Passcode 42

Erase Apple Watch after 10 unlock attempts 43

How to choose language or region on your Watch..................43

How to switch wrists or Digital Crown orientation 44

Staying fit with the Apple Watch 45

Close each ring 46

Initiate a workout routine 47

Use the power of the pedal 48

Tracking important health information on the Watch..............49

Prioritize your sleep with Watch 50

Get heart health notifications 50

Check the oxygen levels of your blood (this is only applicable to Apple Watch Series 6)...51

Tracking your sleep with your Apple Watch 52

How to set up Sleep on Apple Watch...................................53

How to change or turn off your next wake-up alarm 54

How to change or add a sleep schedule 55

How to change sleep options 56

How to view your recent sleep history.................................58

How to measure your blood oxygen levels on Apple Watch (Apple Watch Series 6 only) 59

How to set up Blood Oxygen 60

How to turn off background measurements in sleep mode and theater mode 60

Measure your blood oxygen level.......................................60

How to view your Blood Oxygen measurements history 62

How to set up Apple Watch for a family member 62

Set up your family member's Apple Watch 63

How to set up Screen Time...67

CHAPTER TWO 69

How to open apps on your Apple Watch 69

How to show your apps on a grid or in a list 69

How to open apps from the Home Screen 70

How to open an app from the Dock...................................70

How to choose which apps appear in the Dock 71

How to rearrange your apps in grid view 72

How to Remove an app from Apple Watch 73

How to adjust app settings 73

How to check storage used by apps 74

How to tell time on Apple Watch 74

How to add an alarm on your Apple Watch 75

How to set an alarm on Apple Watch 75

Don't let your alarm snooze 76

How to delete an alarm 77

How to skip a wake-up alarm 78

How to see the same alarms on both your iPhone and Apple Watch . 78

How to set up Apple Watch as a nightstand clock with alarm 79

How to set a timer on Apple Watch 80

How to quickly set a timer 80

How to create a custom timer 81

How to open a stopwatch 81

How to start, stop, and reset your stopwatch 82

How to change the stopwatch format 83

The Apple Watch Status Icon 83

CHAPTER THREE 84

How to use Control Center on your Apple Watch 84

How to open or close Control Center 84

How to rearrange Control Center 85

How to remove Control Center buttons 85

How to turn on the airplane mode on Watch 86

How to use the flashlight on Apple Watch 87

Use theater mode on Apple Watch 88

Disconnect Apple Watch from Wi-Fi 89

How to turn on silent mode 90

How to turn on Do Not Disturb 91

How to turn sleep mode on or off 93

How to locate your iPhone with your Apple Watch 94

How to find your lost Apple Watch 95

Adjusting screen brightness, haptics, sounds, and text size on your Watch 6 and Watch SE. 96

How to adjust brightness and text on Watch 96

How to Adjust Watch sound 97

How to adjust haptic intensity 98

How to turn Digital Crown haptics off or on 99

How to view and respond to notifications on Watch 100

How to quickly respond to notification as they arrive 100

How to see notifications you are yet to attend to 101

Choose how your notifications are delivered 102

How to use notification grouping 104

How to silence all notifications on your Watch 105

How to turn off short look notifications on your Apple Watch is locked 106

How to keep notifications on your Apple Watch private 106

How to use shortcuts on Apple Watch 107

How to run a shortcut 107

How to add a shortcut complication on your watch 107

How to add more shortcuts to Apple Watch 108

Creating an emergency Medical ID with Watch 108

How to set up Medical ID on Watch 109

How to view your Medical ID on Apple Watch 109

Recording an electrocardiogram with your ECG app on Apple Watch 110

How to check heart rate on the Apple Watch 111

See your heart rate 111

Check your heart rate during a workout 112

View a graph of your heart rate data 112

How to turn on your heart rate data 113

By default, the Apple Watch is monitoring your heart rate during; your workout session, for the heart rate app and Breathe sessions. If you have previously turned off the heart rate data; either by mistake or for any other reasons, you can turn it on again buy following the step below; 113

Let Apple Watch control your home. 113

Add a new accessory or scene to the Home app 114

How to control smart home accessories and scenes 115

How to view a different home 115

How to access any of your Smart home accessories remotely with your Apple Watch 116

How to allow remote access 116

How to read mail in the Mail app 116

How to switch to iPhone.. 117

CHAPTER FOUR 120

SOME ESSENTIAL APPLE WATCH APPS........... 120

The Message App on Apple Watch 120

Reading messages on your Apple Watch 120

How to read a message on Apple Watch 120

Check when your messages were sent 121

How to mute or remove a conversation 121

How to access photos, audio, and video in a message 121

Choose how to be notified.. 122

Send messages from Apple Watch.................................... 124

How to create a message on your Apple Watch..................... 124

How to reply to a message... 124

How to send a reply directly to one message in a conversation 125

How to compose a message on your Apple Watch 126

Use Apple Pay to send and receive money 128

Share your location.. 129

How to contact the person you are messaging directly 129

THE MUSIC APP ON YOUR APPLE WATCH 130

Adding music to your Apple Watch 130

How to select which playlists should be added automatically to the Apple Watch 130

How to add albums and playlists to your Apple Watch............ 130

How to add a workout playlist to your Apple Watch 131

View how much music has been stored on your Apple Watch..... 131

How to remove music from your Apple Watch 132

How to play your music on Apple Watch 132

Play music for you 133

The Phone App on Apple Watch...................................... 134

How to answer your call on Watch 134

Things you can do while you are on a call 135

Listening to voicemail on Watch...................................... 136

How to make phone calls on Apple Watch.......................... 137

How to make a call 137

How to input a phone number on the Apple Watch 138

How to send calls over Wi-Fi 138

How to choose a photo album and manage your storage
on Apple Watch 140

How to choose the album you want to store on Apple Watch 140

How to limit photo storage on your Apple Watch 141

How to take a screenshot of Apple Watch 141

How to view your photos on the Apple Watch 142

How to quickly browse photos on your Apple Watch 142

How to view a Live Photo on your Apple Watch 143

How to show a photo on the watch face 143

How to view a photo memory on your Apple Watch 143

CHAPTER FIVE 145

About Apple Watch Wallet 145

Using Apple Pay on the Apple Watch 145

Setting up Apple Pay on your Apple Watch 147

How to add your card to Apple Watch 147

How to choose a default card 148

Reorder payment cards 149

How to delete/remove a card from Apple Pay 149

How to Find the Device Account Number for a card 149

How to change your default transaction details.................... 150

What to do if your Apple Watch is stolen or lost 150

How to pay for a purchase in a store with Apple Watch............ 151

How to make a purchase within an app.............................. 152

About the Author 153

CHAPTER ONE: GETTING READY FOR THE WATCH EXPERIENCE

What is new in apple watch 6 and the apple watch SE?

Apple announced the Watch 6 and the Apple Watch SE at its recent WWDC held in September 2020, but the only thing missing was the iPhone 12 which is expected to be out by October. The Watch 6 and the Apple Watch SE, according to Apple, will both be shipped with the latest Watch OS which is the Watch OS 7; so you don't need to worry about updating your Watch to the latest Watch OS. The Watch OS 7 running on the Watch 6 and SE comes with a lot of mouthwatering features and awe-inspiring looks. You will be able to pair your Apple Watch with iPhone running the latest iOS 14. The following are list of iPhones (iOS 14) that can be paired with the Watch 6 and SE; 1st generation of iPhone SE, iPhone SE (2020 Model), iPhone XS, iPhone XS Max, iPhone XR, iPhone 11, iPhone 11 Pro, iPhone 11 Pro Max, iPhone 8, iPhone 8 Plus, iPhone 7, iPhone 7 Plus, iPhone 6s and iPhone 6s Plus. Also, the much rumored iPhone 12 (will run on iOS 14) will also pair with the Apple Watch. The Apple Watch 6 and SE came with a lot of useful functions and apps which make them a little bit different from the previous Apple Watches; all thanks to the Watch OS 7 update.

Here are what is new on Apple Watch 6 and SE;

- **You can now share your Watch Face with Face sharing**: The latest Watch OS 7 on Apple Watch 6 & SE lets you share the face of your Watch with a friend or some other persons. There are also improved and customized Watch faces that are available for download on the Apple Store.
- **You can now track how well you sleep with the sleep tracking**: Wear your Watch even while you are sleeping and keep track of how you sleep each night. The Apple Watch 6 and SE are packed with a Watch accelerometer that can sense the way you respire as you sleep. Your Watch is able to smartly capture when its wearer is sleeping and the length of period you used to sleep each night. When you wake up, you will see data of your previous night's sleep and the time of sleep and wake.

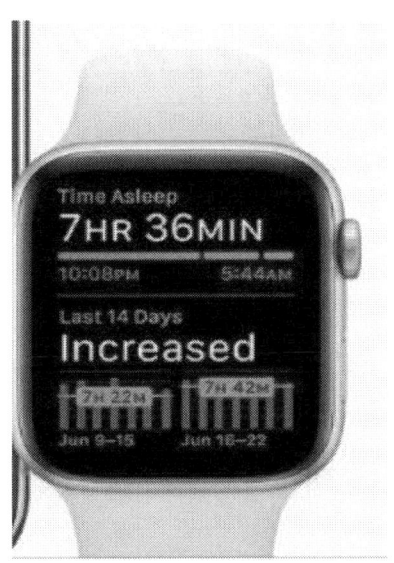

- **Smart Hand washing detection**: The updated hand washing detection on Watch OS 7 will monitor you while washing your hands. The Watch uses the combination of its motion sensor, on-device learning and microphone to know when you are washing your hands. As soon as the Watch observes that you are washing your hand, a 20 - seconds timer will be prompted on the screen to guide you to wash your hands for the right amount of time. If you stop washing when it is not yet time to stop, the Watch will prompt you to keep washing your hands. On returning home from a long journey, your Watch will also remind you to wash your hands. In this period of Coronavirus pandemic, how better should Apple cares?

- **Hearing**: The human ear has a particular level of noises that it can accommodate at a time so that you don't get to damage your hearing. Your Apple Watch 6 comes with a noise app that allows users to know when they are in a noisy environment. The new Watch OS (Watch OS 7) has already improved on this. Whenever you are listening to music too loud for your eardrum, your device will issue a warning so that you can reduce the volume of the sound.
- **Fitness App**: This is your go-to app where you can get your daily activity data.
- **Manage your kids' or other family members' Apple Watch**: The new Watch OS 7 on Apple Watch 6 and SE allows you to setup and manage your kids' Apple Watch and that of other family members through the Family Sharing group.
- **How do you prompt Siri on Apple Watch to give you translation of words or how to say some words or statements in other languages**: You can ask your Watch "How do you say Good Morning in Chinese?"
- **Measure your blood oxygen level (for Watch 6 only):** You can now measure the level of oxygen in your blood with the Watch 6. The Blood Oxygen app on your Watch will help you to achieve this by measuring the percentage of oxygen carried from the lung to other part of your body.

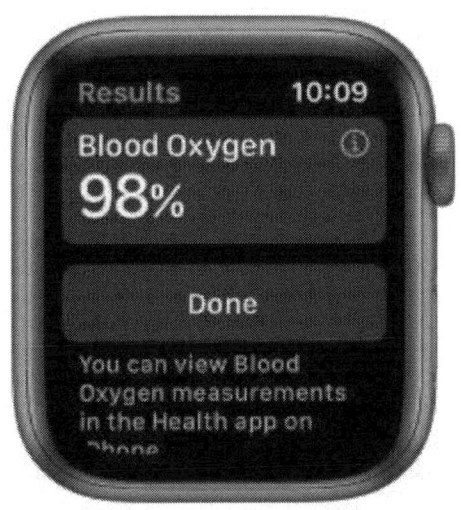

How to set up and pair your Apple Watch with iPhone

To maximally utilize your Apple Watch 6 or SE with WatchOS 7, you will need to pair your Watch with an iPhone 6s or some other later versions with the new iOS 14 or 13.4 or less.

How to turn on, pair, and set up your Apple Watch

1. Place the Apple Watch SE or the Apple Watch 6 on your wrist. You can adjust the Watch band or select a proper band size so that the Apple Watch will fit perfectly and look nice on your wrist. The band on your Apple Watch must be one that corresponds with the size of your

Watch. Using another band watch that doesn't correspond with your watch might not help when you want to fasten the watch on your wrist. For reference sake, you will be able to use Apple Watch band designed for older watch series (like the watch series 1, watch series 2, watch series 3 and the Apple Watch 1st generation) with your Apple Watch 6 and Apple Watch SE as the sizes seem to be compatible. In the same vein, you can use the Apple Watch band designed for your Apple Watch SE and Apple Watch 6 on previous Apple Watch series like the Apple Watch 4 and 5. The solo Loop and the braided loop can also work with your Apple Watch 6 and Apple Watch SE as they are made specifically for the Apple Watch 4, 5, 6 and SE. If you plan to remove your watch band anytime soon, simply follow the instructions below;

1. Press the release button of the band on your Watch.
2. Slide the Watch band across and then slide in the new Watch band. The Apple Watch should be adjusted so that it fits perfectly on your Wrist. This is because features like haptic notifications, heart rate sensor and wrist detection work better when your Apple watch is directly making contact with your skin. In fact, the sensor works properly only when you wear Apple Watch on the top of your wrist.

2. Turn on the Apple Watch 6 and SE by pressing and holding the Watch side button till the Apple logo comes up.

3. Position your iPhone (iPhone that can work with iOS 14 like the iPhone 6S or later iPhone series) near the Apple Watch 6 and SE, you will see the Apple Watch pairing screen on your iPhone, tap continue. You can, alternatively, launch the Apple Watch app on your iPhone 6S or later and then click on "Pair New Watch."

4. When asked, position the iPhone to let your Apple Watch shows up in the viewfinder in your Apple Watch app. This will pair the Apple Watch with the iPhone.

5. Click on "Set Up Apple Watch." And then follow the on-screen instructions on your Apple Watch and iPhone for complete setup.

Hint: If you are having trouble pairing your Apple Watch with the method discussed above, you can set up the Watch using VoiceOver. Follow the steps below to automatically or manually (if automatic fails to work) set up your Watch with the VoiceOver;

How to set up Apple Watch using VoiceOver

1. Activate your Apple Watch (turn it on) by pressing on the side button located below the Watch's Digital Crown.

2. Click on the Digital Crown three times to turn on the VoiceOver on your Apple Watch.

3. Bring the Apple Watch and your iPhone very close to each other.

4. Tap on Continue on your iPhone and then double tap.

5. Again, select "Set Up Apple Watch," and then double-tap.

6. You can automatically pair your Watch and iPhone by pointing your iPhone camera towards the watch from around 5 to 6 inches away. Upon hearing the pairing confirmation, set up your watch by following the spoken prompts. In case you experience difficulty while pairing your Apple Watch with your iPhone using the automatic pairing, you can try the manual pairing from step 7 to 13.

7. Tap on "Set up Apple Watch Manually," on your iPhone and then double-tap.

8. Click on the info button on the Apple Watch located at the bottom right side of the watch and then double tap.

9. You will see your Apple Watch unique identifier located near the top of the watch's screen. The unique identifier for your Watch might sound like "Apple Watch 58953."

10. Select the exact unique identifier on your iPhone and then double tap.

11. You can tap on the six-digit pairing code on the Apple Watch to listen to it.

12. Input this pairing code from the Apple Watch on your iPhone by using the iPhone's keyboard.

    Upon successful pairing, you sense a tap coming from your Apple Watch saying "Your Apple Watch is paired." If the pairing is not successful, click on the notification alert to respond, and both devices will reset so that you can give it another shot.

13. On your iPhone device, select "Restore from Backup" or "Set up as New Apple Watch," and then double-tap.

Continue the set up process by following the spoken prompts. Upon successful setup of your Apple Watch, the Watch will synchronize with your iPhone and you will need to wait a few moments. When you hear the "sync complete," the Watch is ready to be used and the Watch Face will comes up. Swipe left or right on the screen to start exploring the features of the Apple Watch Face.

As part of the setup process, you can enable cellular service on the Apple Watch by following the steps below;

Using Apple Watch 6 with cellular

The Apple Watch 6 with cellular (GPS + Cellular) together with a cellular connection using the same carrier on your iPhone can be used to stream music, sends calls, reply to messages, use Walkie-Talkie, receives notifications and a lot more even when your iPhone is not currently with you. The cellular service on Apple Watch is not available in all regions.

How to activate/Add Apple Watch to your cellular plan

If you didn't activate the Apple Watch cellular plan during the initial setting up of your Apple Watch, you can still do it now by following the prompts below;

- Launch the Apple Watch app on your iPhone (iPhone 6S or later)
- Click on "My Watch," and then select "Cellular."

How to turn on/off cellular service on Apple Watch

The Apple Watch 6 with cellular deploys the best connection it sees around. This can be your iPhone's connection when they are near each other, a secured Wi-Fi network that you have safely connected to in the past or a cellular connection. Turning off cellular connection on your Apple Watch will help to conserve battery power and makes it last.

- Tap and hold the bottom of your Watch's screen and then swipe up to launch the Control Center.
- Click on ((*)) and then turn on or off cellular network.

The cellular button will usually turns green anytime your Apple Watch is safely connected to a network and your iPhone is not within reach.

How to check the data usage used by your Watch

- Launch the Apple Watch app on the iPhone (iPhone 6S or later).
- Click on "My Watch," and then select "Cellular."

Although, your iPhone and the Watch must be connected with the same carrier but you can actually used a different carrier from the one you are using on the iPhone paired with the Watch if you set up the Watch for your family member.

How to remove your cellular plan

1. Launch the Apple Watch app on your device.

2. Click on "My Watch," select "Cellular," and then click on the ⓘ located next to your cellular plan.

3. Click on "Remove [*name of carrier*] Plan," and then confirm.

   You may be required to make contact with your carrier in order to remove your Apple Watch from the cellular plan.

Are you having trouble pairing your Watch?

- Are you seeing a Watch Face during pairing even when you are not sure whether you have paired your Watch with another iPhone before? Seeing a Watch Face means that the Apple Watch has been paired with an iPhone. If you are not sure which iPhone has been paired, you can consider erasing all Apple Watch contents and reset your settings.

How to erase Apple Watch and settings

1. From the Apple Watch, launch the Settings app .

2. Scroll to General, click on "Reset," and then choose "Erase All Content and Settings," and then input your passcode.

   If you have already set up cellular connection on your Apple Watch, you will be prompted with two options; Erase All and Erase All & Keep Plan. If you choose the "Erase all," you will be able to erase your Apple Watch completely. The "Erase All & Keep Plan" helps you to erase your Watch and you can later restore with your cellular plan.

Alternatively, launch the Apple Watch app on your iPhone, click on "My Watch," scroll to "General," tap "Reset" and then choose "Erase Apple Watch Content and Settings."

In case you are unable to navigate the settings app on your Watch probably because you cannot remember the passcode, simply place the Watch on its charger and then click and hold the Watch's side button to bring Power Off. Press and then hold on the digital crown and then select Reset."

After you have successfully reset your Apple Watch and the Watch restarts, you will have to pair the Watch again with your own iPhone by following the instructions above.

- Your Camera cannot initiate the pairing? Select "Pair Apple Watch Manually" prompted at the lower side of your iPhone screen, and then follows the onscreen instructions.

- If your Apple Watch is not pairing with iPhone: A red iPhone icon on the Apple Watch is a sign that your Apple Watch connection has not been established, and you can try to reconnect both devices again.

    o Check your Apple Watch connection

If you cannot receive messages, notifications, or calls on the Apple Watch, it is possible that the Apple Watch and iPhone are not properly connected. When both devices disconnect, you will see the red iPhone icon 📱 or the red X icon ❌ coming up on your watch face. When the Apple Watch reconnects, you will see a green iPhone icon 📱 on the Watch Face.

To reestablish connection, bring the paired iPhone very close to the Apple Watch. If this does not solve the problem, you can try any of the two procedures below;

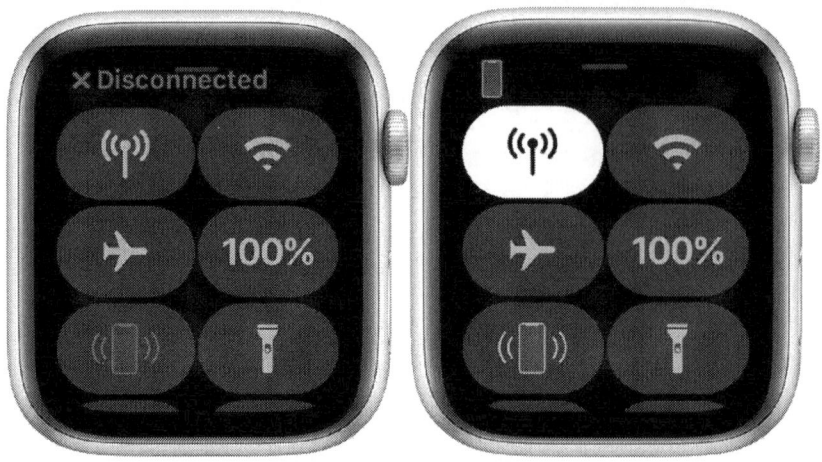

1. Make a move to connect your Apple Watch and iPhone again
2. Make sure your iPhone and the Apple Watch are in range by bringing the Apple Watch close to the paired iPhone.
3. Ensure that the Bluetooth and the Wi-Fi are enabled on the iPhone and the Airplane mode is disabled. You can launch the Control Center to confirm.

4. If the Airplane Mode icon ✈ shows on the watch face, it means the Airplane Mode is on. Launch the Control Center to turn off the Airplane Mode.
5. Restart the Apple Watch and the iPhone.
6. Unpair your devices, then pair them again

If, after following the steps above, your device cannot still to connect, you can consider unpairing it from the iPhone and then pair it again with the iPhone.

How to unpair Apple Watch

1. Launch the Apple Watch app on the iPhone.
2. Click on "My Watch," and then click on "All Watches" located at the top of the screen.
3. Select ⓘ beside the Apple Watch that you want to unpair and then select "Unpair Apple Watch."

How to pair more than one Apple Watch

You can actually pair more than one Apple Watches – say Apple Watch 6 and Apple Watch SE – on your iPhone just the exact same way you paired the first Apple Watch. Follow the steps below;

1. Launch the Apple Watch app on the iPhone.

2. Click on "My Watch," and then click on "All Watches" located at the top of the screen.

3. Select "Pair New Watch," and then follow the instructions on the screen to start pairing.

How to quickly switch to a different Apple Watch

Your iPhone is able to detect the paired Apple Watch on your Wrist and will connect to it automatically. Just wear a different Apple Watch (after you have pair it with the procedure above) and raise your Wrist a bit.

You can as well manually choose an Apple Watch;

1. Launch the Apple Watch app on the iPhone.

2. Click on "My Watch," and then click on "All Watches" located at the top of the screen.

3. Disable Auto Switch by turning it off.

To confirm if the Apple Watch has been connected to your iPhone, touch and then hold the bottom of your Watch screen, swipe the screen up to access the Control Center and then check to see the "Connected status icon ▯ " Under the Auto Switch menu, the active Apple Watch will be shown by a yellow mark at the side of the Watch while other Watches will be shown below the active Watch.

How to pair Apple Watch to a new iPhone

If you have previously paired your Apple Watch to an old iPhone (say iPhone 11) and you now want to pair with a new device (say the new iPhone 12 to be released by October 2020), kindly follow the steps below;

1. Backup the old iPhone you are currently pairing with your Watch by using the iCloud.

2. Set up the new iPhone. On the iPhone's Apps & Data screen, select to restore your device from an iCloud backup and then choose the latest backup.

3. Continue setting up your and, when asked, you can then choose to utilize your Apple Watch with the new iPhone.

When you have successfully set up your iPhone, the Apple Watch will ask you to pair the Apple Watch to the new iPhone. Select OK on the Apple Watch and then input its passcode.

How to transfer an existing cellular plan to a new Apple Watch

You will be able to transfer your existing cellular plan from the Apple Watch 5 with cellular to another Apple Watch with cellular, say Apple Watch 6 with cellular by following the steps below;

1. Wear the Apple Watch on your wrist and launch the Apple Watch app on the iPhone.

2. Click on "My Watch," select "Cellular," and then click on ⓘ next to the cellular plan.

   Click on "Remove [*name of carrier*] Plan," and then confirm. You may be required to contact your carrier in order to remove your Apple Watch from the cellular plan.

3. Remove the old watch, wear the other Apple Watch with cellular, click on "My Watch," and then select "Cellular."

   Follow the instructions to activate your watch for cellular.

How to charge Apple Watch

- Set up your Apple Watch Charger

- o Place the Apple Watch magnetic charging cable or the Apple Watch charging dock that came with the Watch on a flat surface.
- o Plug the dock or the charging cable into the power adaptor. The power adaptor will not come with the Apple Watch as it is sold separately.
- o Plug the Power Adaptor into a secured power outlet.

- **Begin to charge the Apple Watch**
  - o Position the magnetic charging cable on the back of the Watch. The concave end of your charging cable will magnetically snap to the back of your Watch and align itself properly. A chime sound is given off when charging starts. You will also see the charging symbol ⚡ on the face of the Watch. You will see this symbol ⚡ if your battery is low.

Check the time you last charge your Apple Watch

1. Launch the Settings app ⚙ on the Apple Watch.
2. Click on "Battery."

You will be prompted with the battery screen showing you the battery percentage that is remaining on the Apple Watch, a simple graph detailing the recent charge history and the time you last charge the battery.

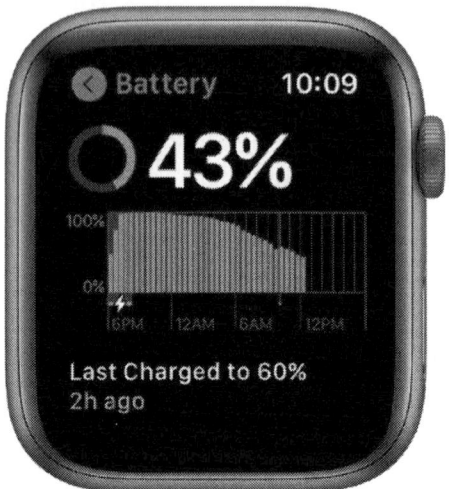

You can as well use your iPhone to confirm the last charge time of the Watch. To do this, launch the Apple Watch app on the iPhone, select "My Watch," tap on "General" and select "Usage."

How to know your Watch's battery health

You will be able to check the power of the Watch battery and the compare it with what you used to have when then Watch was new.

1. Launch the Settings app on the Apple Watch.

2. Click on "Battery," and then select "Battery Health."

To prevent your Watch's battery from aging fast, Apple Watch tries to understand your charging routines so that it won't be consuming battery on its own until it charges up to 80% of the battery, unless there is need for you to use it.

Apple Watch will always notify you if the battery capacity is reduced so that you can check what is causing this.

How to Lock or unlock Apple Watch

How to unlock Apple Watch

Apple Watch can be unlocked by manual method (entering your passcode) and you can as well set the Watch to automatically unlock anytime you unlock your iPhone.

- Manually unlock Apple Watch by entering passcode: Wake up Apple Watch, input the passcode for the Watch and then select OK.

- Use your iPhone to unlock Watch: Launch the Settings app on the Apple Watch, click on "Passcode," and then enable the "Unlock with iPhone" by turning it on. If you don't want to launch settings app on your Watch, you can as well use your iPhone to unlock the Watch automatically by launching the Watch app on the iPhone, click on "Passcode" and then turn on the "Unlock with iPhone" feature. The iPhone and the Apple Watch must be within acceptable Bluetooth range (say about 9 to 10 meters) from each other to be able to unlock the Apple Watch. If your Bluetooth is disabled on the Watch, input the passcode on the Watch to unlock the Bluetooth.

Tip: It is not acceptable (for security reasons) for you to use the same passcode on your Watch and iPhone. If you can, try and make use of different passcode for both as there are many passcode as possible to go around.

How to change passcode on the Apple Watch

If you feel your passcode has been compromised, you should try to change your initial passcode to a new one unknown to anyone. To do this, simply follow the steps below;

1. Launch the Settings app on the Apple Watch.

2. Select "Passcode," click on "Change Passcode" and then follow the onscreen guides.

You can as well use your iPhone to change passcode for the Apple Watch;

- Launch the Apple Watch app from your iPhone
- Click on "My Watch," click on passcode, select "Change Passcode" and follow the instructions on the screen. .

Trick: You might not be able to use passcode longer than four digits on your Apple Watch, but if you wish to use a passcode longer than 4 digits, there is a way you can go about it. Simply launch your Settings app on the Apple Watch, select "Passcode" and turn off simple Passcode.

How to disable Passcode if you don't want to use it to unlock your Watch.

1. Launch the Settings app ⚙ on the Watch SE or Watch 6.

2. Click on "Passcode," and then select "Turn Passcode Off."

You can as well use your iPhone to turn off Passcode for the Watch by launching the Apple Watch on the iPhone, click on "My Watch," select "Passcode" and then choose "Turn Passcode Off."

Advise: Do not disable Passcode on the Watch if you still want to enjoy Apple Pay on the Watch and also for security reasons.

How to lock Watch automatically

Your Apple Watch, by default, will actually lock automatically when it is not on your Wrist. You can change this Wrist detection feature from Apple Watch settings. To do this;

1. Launch the Settings app ⚙ on the Watch.

2. Click on "Passcode," and then choose to turn on or turn off Wrist Detection.

The following Watch's features are automatically affected when you turn off your Watch's Wrist detection;

- The Apple Pay will now be asking you to input the Passcode anytime you click twice on the Side button to authorize payment.

- Some Activity measurements will not be accessible.

- The Heart rate tracking feature and notifications will be turned off.

- The Apple Watch will no longer be able to lock and unlock automatically.

- The Watch SE, Watch 6 and later Watch series won't be able to send an emergency call even after the Watch detects a hard fall.

How to lock your Watch manually

1. Launch the Control Center by touching and holding the bottom of the Watch's screen.

2. Click on 🔒.

3. Note: To unlock your Watch manually, you will have to turn off the Wrist Detection feature by launching the Settings app ⚙ on the Watch, click on "Passcode," and then choose to turn off Wrist Detection.

You will need to use your Passcode the next time you are using Apple Watch.

To avoid unintended tap when you are working out or during exercise, you will have to lock your Watch's screen. While you are deploying the Workout app 🏃 on the Apple Watch, simply swipe right and then click on "Lock." When you are on a swimming workout, the Apple Watch will automatically lock your screen with Water Lock.

What to do when you forget your Passcode

If you cannot remember your Apple Watch Passcode for one reason or another, you will have to erase the Apple Watch. This can be done by any of the following methods;

- Unpair the Watch from your iPhone to erase the Watch settings and passcode and you can then pair the Watch again with iPhone.
- Carry out Apple Watch reset and then pair Watch again with the iPhone.

You can reset Apple Watch by using the methods discussed in the previous lesson.

Erase Apple Watch after 10 unlock attempts

You can protect Watch from theft by setting the Watch to erase all contents after ten (10) unwarranted attempts to unlock the Watch with a wrong Passcode. To do this, follow the steps below;

1. Launch the Settings app on the Watch.

2. Click on "Passcode," and then turn on the "Erase Data."

How to choose language or region on your Watch

1. Launch your Apple Watch app on iPhone.

2. Select "My Watch," scroll to General, select "Language & Region," choose "Custom," and then select "Watch Language."

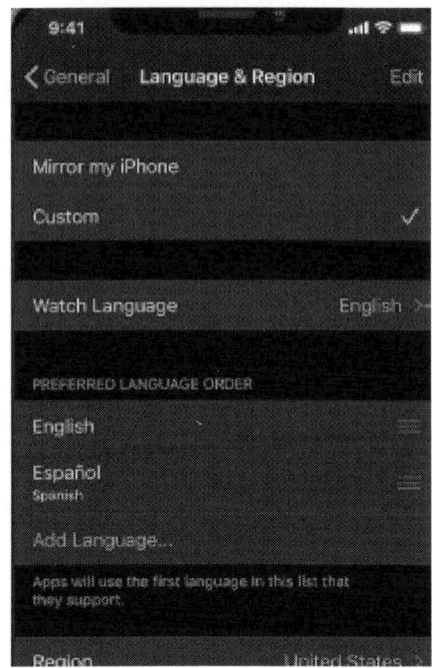

How to switch wrists or Digital Crown orientation

If you plan to move the Watch to your other wrist or you just want the Digital Crown to be on the other side, you can adjust the orientation settings so that you will be able to wake Watch by raising your wrist, and you will can move things in any direction by turning the Digital Crown. To do this;

1. Launch the Settings app ⚙ on the Apple Watch.

2. Scroll to General and click on "Orientation."

You can as well launch the Apple Watch app on iPhone, select "My Watch," then scroll to General and tap "Watch Orientation."

Staying fit with the Apple Watch

The Apple Watch is your perfect fitness companion as it helps monitor workouts and activities to teach you how to live a more productive life with quick reminders and healthy human-app competition.

Close each ring

The Apple Watch can help tracks how you move, how much you stand up, and how well you are able to exercise every day. Set fitness goals in your Activity app ⊚ while monitoring your daily progress. Go down the apps to see more details like your total distance and dance moves. The Watch will notify when you completed a set goal.

Initiate a workout routine

Launch the Workout app and then choose the category of workout that you want—like swimming, running, or dancing. You will be able to see your workout statistics on a single screen to help monitor progress at a glance. If you do not remember to start your workout before exercising, don't fret—Apple Watch will suggest that you launch the Workout app and gives credit for the exercise you have already finished.

Use the power of the pedal

With the perks of the watchOS 7, the Apple Watch has make it especially very easier now than ever to work out on two wheels by prompting you with cycling directions—bringing you maps that display elevation changes, busy roads and bike lanes.

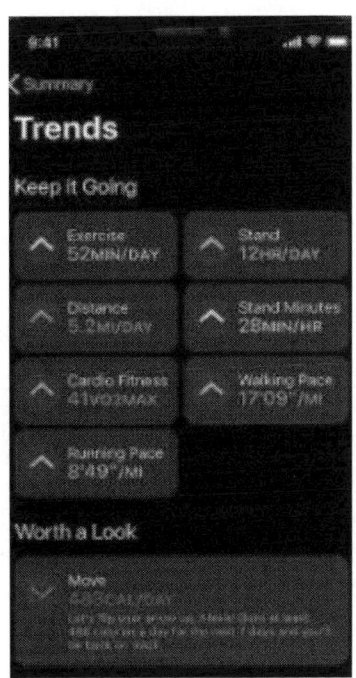

Tracking important health information on the Watch

The Apple Watch can guide you to meet sleep goals, measure blood oxygen level, guide you to safely wash your hands and monitor useful health information related to the health.

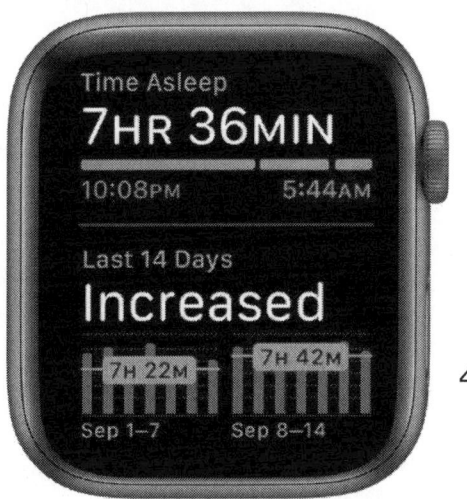

Prioritize your sleep with Watch

With Apple Watch, you can create a sleep schedule, monitor how well you sleep each day and report your sleeping schedule over the course of time. To begin, launch the Health app on your iPhone and then create a sleep schedule. Then wear the Watch on your wrist when you want to sleep and the Watch takes up from here.

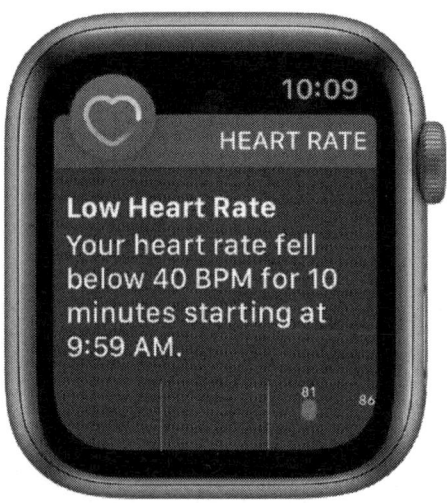

Get heart health notifications

You can allow notifications from the Heart Rate app on the Watch to tell you to increase or reduce heart rates. The irregular heart rhythm notification on the Watch will also let you know if notices an irregular rhythm suggestive of Atrial fibrillation. Launch the Apple Watch app on iPhone, scroll to "My Watch," and then click on "Heart." Enable High Heart Rate or Low Heart Rate by turning them on, set your heart rate threshold and also turn on the irregular rhythm notifications.

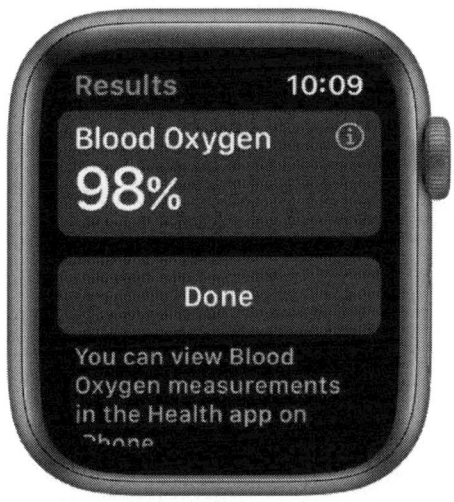

Check the oxygen levels of your blood (this is only applicable to Apple Watch Series 6)

Deploy the Blood Oxygen app on the Watch to measure your blood's oxygen level straight from your wrist. View the most recent Watch's measurement and see a record of all the readings in your Health app on the iPhone.

Tracking your sleep with your Apple Watch

Meet your sleep goals with the Sleep app 🛏 on your Watch by creating achievable bedtime plans. While going to bed, place your Watch on any of your wrist so that Apple Watch will be able to monitor how well you slept. On waking up, launch the Sleep app to check how well you sleep and monitor your sleep trend over the past two weeks. You will be asked to charge the Watch once the battery is less than 30% before you retire to bed. When you wake up, just take a look at the screen to check how much charge (of the battery percentage) is left.

If you want, you can actually create multiple sleeping schedules—for instance, one sleeping schedule for weekdays and another one for weekends. For each of the sleeping schedule, you will be able to set up the following:

- Your sleep goal (how many hours, per day, of sleep you plan to get)

- The actual time you want to be retiring to bed and the time you want to be waking up

- A beautiful alarm sound to help you wake up at the appropriate time.

- When to enable the sleep mode. The sleep mode helps limit multiple distractions before you retire to bed and allow you to have satisfactory sleep once you are in bed.

- Sleep tracking, capable of using your motion to notice sleep when your Watch is in sleep mode and when you, of course, wear it to bed.

Tip: To leave sleep mode, turn the Watch's Digital Crown to unlock and then swipe up the screen to launch Control Center and click on .

How to set up Sleep on Apple Watch

1. Launch your Sleep app on the Watch.

2. Proceed to set up by following the onscreen instructions.

You can as well use the Health app on your iPhone, select Browse, click on "Sleep," and then choose "Get Started (you will see the "Get started" under Set Up Sleep)."

How to change or turn off your next wake-up alarm

1. Launch the Sleep app on your Watch.

2. Select by tapping your current bedtime.

3. You can initiate a new wake-up time by tapping on the wake-up time, turn the Watch's Digital Crown to initiate a new time and then choose "Set."

If you don't like the idea of your Watch waking you up in the morning, you can disable the alarm.

The changes you enabled is only applicable to your next wake-up alarm.

Note: You will also be able to turn off your next wake-up alarm from the Alarms app . Simply click on the alarm that shows under Sleep | Wake up and then select "Skip for Tonight."

How to change or add a sleep schedule

1. Launch the Sleep app on your Watch.
2. Click on "Full Schedule," and then carry out one of the following;

- *Change a sleep schedule:* Click on your current sleep schedule.

- *Add a sleep schedule:* Click on "Add Another Schedule."

- *Change your sleep goal:* Click on "Sleep Goal," and proceed to set the amount of time you wish to sleep.

- *Change Wind Down time:* Click on "Wind Down," and then set the amount of time you plan for the sleep mode to be on active mode before your bedtime.

You can minimize distractions before your planned bedtime when sleep mode activates during Wind Down. The Sleep mode actually turns off your watch display and activates the "Do Not Disturb."

Carry out any of these;

- *Set the days for your schedule:* Select your schedule, click on the area beneath Active On. Pick days and then click on "Done."

- *Adjust your wake time and bedtime:* Select "Wake Up or Bedtime," turn your Watch's Digital Crown to initiate a new time and then choose Set.

- *Set the alarm options:* You will be able to turn on/off Alarm and choose Sound to select your Alarm sound.

- *Remove or cancel a sleep schedule:* Click on "Delete Schedule (located at the bottom end of your Watch's screen)" to erase an existing schedule, or click on "Cancel (located at the top of your Watch screen)" to cancel the process of creating a new sleep schedule.

How to change sleep options

1. Launch the Settings app ⚙ on the Apple Watch.

2. Click on "Sleep," and proceed to turn off/on any of the options below;

   - *Sleep Mode:* Sleep mode helps to simplify your Lock screen at the scheduled Wind Down time you set. The Sleep mode will turn on by default. If you plan to have control over this option, click on Sleep Mode and then turn off the feature.

   - *Show time:* Bring the correct date and time on the iPhone and your Apple Watch during sleep mode. Click on "Sleep Mode" to turn on/off this feature.

   - *Sleep Tracking::* By turning on this feature, Watch will monitor your sleep and help you include sleep data in the health app on your iPhone.

   - *Charging reminders:* Your Watch is able to remind you to charge your Watch before the Wind Down time and will also tells you when the Watch has been fully charged.

   - *Wake to haptic taps:* Touch the bottom of the Watch Screen, hold and swipe up the screen to launch the Control Center. Click on 🔔 to enable silent mode. Your Watch will wake you up with taps without audible alarm.

You can also use your iPhone to change these settings and some other sleep options. To do this, launch your Health app on iPhone, click on "Browse," and then scroll to Sleep > Options.

How to view your recent sleep history

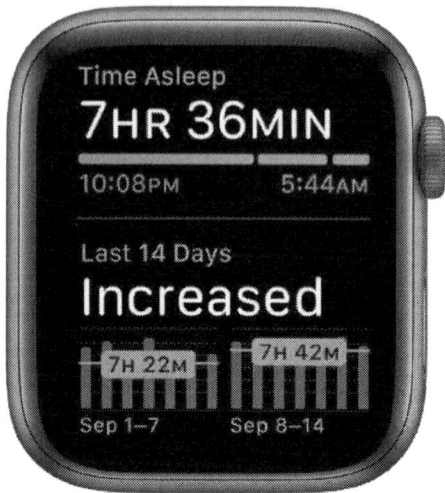

1. Launch the Sleep app on the Apple Watch.

2. Scroll down on the screen to check the amount of sleep you had the previous night and your average sleep over the last two weeks.

To view the sleep history on your iPhone, launch the Health app on your iPhone, click on "Browse," and then select Sleep.

How to measure your blood oxygen levels on Apple Watch (Apple Watch Series 6 only)

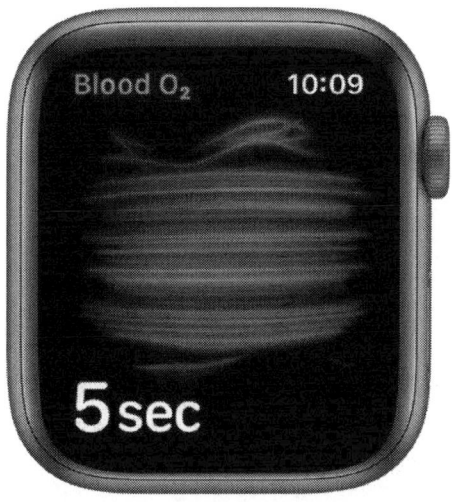

You can now measure the level of oxygen in your blood with the Watch 6. The Blood Oxygen app on your Watch will help you to achieve this by measuring the percentage of oxygen carried from the lung to other part of your body. When you know how well your blood is oxygenated, you will be able to get a glimpse of your overall health and wellbeing.

Note: The Blood Oxygen app does not work in all regions. Do not use the Blood Oxygen app measurements for serious medical use. Consult your doctor if you are not well.

How to set up Blood Oxygen

1. Launch the Apple Watch app on iPhone (for iPhone 6s users or later with iOS 14).

2. Click on "My Watch," select "Blood Oxygen," and then proceed to turn on the Blood Oxygen Measurements.

How to turn off background measurements in sleep mode and theater mode

The Blood oxygen measurements utilize a bright red light which shines against your wrist. The red light may appear more profound in dark places. If you don't like the red light from this feature, you can disable measurements.

1. Launch the Settings app on the Apple Watch.

2. Select "Blood Oxygen," and proceed to turn it off In Sleep Mode and In Theater Mode.

Measure your blood oxygen level

When you enabled the background measurement, the Blood Oxygen app is able to periodically measure the level of oxygen in your blood throughout the day. Notwithstanding, you will be able to take instant measurement anytime you want it.

1. Launch the Blood Oxygen app on the Watch.

2. Place your arm on a good table or on your lap, and ensure that your wrist is flat while you let the Watch's display to be facing up.

3. Select "Start," and let your arm be in still mode during the period. This will only takes fifteen (15) minutes.

4. The result of your blood oxygen level will come up once the measurement is completed. Click on "Done" to finish.

Tricks: For better results, let the back of the Watch be in close contact with your skin. In the same vein, you need to wear the Watch not to tight and not too loose equally; to ensure perfect blood oxygen measurement.

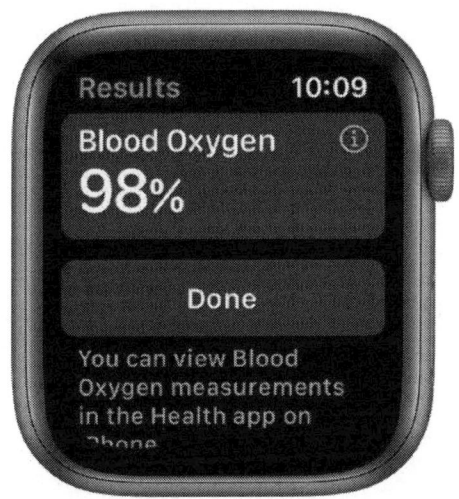

How to view your Blood Oxygen measurements history

1. Launch the Health app on iPhone.

2. Select "Browse," click on "Respiratory," and then select "Blood Oxygen."

How to set up Apple Watch for a family member

If you have an underage kid or parents who probably do not have their own Apple Watch, you can set up Apple Watch for them on your own iPhone. To do this, you need to be the organizer in the Family Sharing group.

The iPhone you initially used to pair and set up Apple Watch have to be within reasonable Bluetooth range (about 10 meters) of the Apple Watch you want to use to manage settings and update the Watch software. The family member that you want to set up the Watch for must be member of your Family Sharing group and must be in possession of cellular-enabled Apple Watch SE or Apple Watch 6. Note that it is not compulsory that your family member's Watch use the same cellular network as the iPhone you want to be managing it with (probably your own iPhone in this case).

By deploying the Apple Watch app and the screen time on your own iPhone, you will be able to manage the following features;

- The limit with which they use the Apple Watch to communicate.

- Screen time away schedule. This lets you choose what time their Watch screen will be active so that they will not be wasting too much time playing with their Watch.

- Schooltime— Set a feature that restricts some Apple Watch features from functioning during school hours

- Place restrictions on some explicit contents, privacy and purchases.

Also, you will be able to access Activity, location information and Health for the Apple Watch you are managing depending on the set up.

Note: The Apple Watch that you set up for your child or any of your family member will be limited in few of its interaction with the iPhone that you used to set it up. For instance, you won't be able to unlock a paired iPhone from the Watch you set up for your kid or a family member. In the same vein, deleting an app from a set up Apple Watch (for a family member) will not remove such app from the iPhone that was used to set it up. An Apple Watch set up for a family member is limited in some of its interactions with.

Set up your family member's Apple Watch

The way you set up a family member's Apple Watch is identical to the same way you set up Apple Watch for yourself. Before pairing and setting up a Watch for your kid or family member, be sure to erase the Apple Watch so that the Watch will not hae any content. The procedure for erasing Apple

Watch has been discussed in the previous chapter. To set up Watch for family member, follow the guides below;

1. Ask your kid or family member to put on their Apple Watch (by fastening the Watch to their wrist). They should adjust the Watch's band or get a comfortable band size so that the Watch will fit well on their wrist. The procedures for changing Watch band have been discussed in the previous chapter.

2. Turn on the Apple Watch 6 and SE by pressing and holding the Watch side button till the Apple logo comes up.

3. Position your iPhone (iPhone that can work with iOS 14 like the iPhone 6S or later iPhone series) near your family member's Apple Watch 6 and SE, you will see the Apple Watch pairing screen on your iPhone, tap continue. You can, alternatively, launch the Apple Watch app on your iPhone 6S or later and then click on "Pair New Watch."

4. Click on "Set Up for a Family Member," and then select "Continue" on the next screen.

5. When asked, position the iPhone to let your Apple Watch shows up in the viewfinder in your Apple Watch app. This will pair the Apple Watch with the iPhone.

6. Click on "Set Up Apple Watch." And then follow the on-screen instructions on your Apple Watch and iPhone for complete setup.

If you are having difficulty setting up watch for your family member, you can use the VoiceOver to either automatically or manually set up Apple Watch for your child or family member. To do this;

14. Activate their Apple Watch (turn it on) by pressing on the side button located below the Watch's Digital Crown.

15. Click on the Digital Crown three times to turn on the VoiceOver on their Apple Watch.

16. Bring the Apple Watch and your iPhone very close to each other.

17. Tap on Continue on your iPhone and then double tap.

18. Again, select "Set Up Apple Watch," and then double-tap.

19. You can automatically pair their Watch and your iPhone by pointing your iPhone camera towards the watch from around 5 to 6 inches away. Upon hearing the pairing confirmation, set up their Watch by following the spoken prompts. In case you experience difficulty while pairing their Apple Watch with your iPhone using the automatic pairing, you can try the manual pairing from step 7 to 13.

20. Tap on "Set up Apple Watch Manually," on your own iPhone and then double-tap.

21. Click on the info button on the Apple Watch located at the bottom right side of the watch and then double tap.

22. You will see their Apple Watch unique identifier located near the top of their watch's screen. The unique identifier for their Watch might sound like "Apple Watch 45998."

23. Select the exact unique identifier on your own iPhone and then double tap.

24. You can tap on the six-digit pairing code on your kid's or family member's Apple Watch to listen to it.

25. Input this pairing code from their Apple Watch on your own iPhone by using the iPhone's keyboard.

Upon successful pairing, you sense a tap coming from their Apple Watch saying "Your Apple Watch is paired." If the pairing is not successful, click on the notification alert to respond, and both devices will reset so that you can give it another shot.

26. On your iPhone device, select "Restore from Backup" or "Set up as New Apple Watch," and then double-tap.

Continue the set up process by following the spoken prompts. Upon successful setup of your kid's or family member's Apple Watch, the Watch will synchronize with your iPhone and you will need to wait a few moments. When you hear the "sync complete," the Watch is ready to be used and the Watch Face will comes up. Ask them to swipe left or right on their screen to start exploring the features of the Apple Watch Face.

You can also enable cellular service on their Apple Watch for them.

How to set up Screen Time

The Screen time feature on Apple Watch can be deployed to set up controls for your family member's Apple Watch. Using the Screen time feature, you can set time away from screen for them, restrict contacts and apps that they can use for communication, limit what they can get and buy from the iTunes Stores and App Store. Also, you will be able to control their access to explicit contents and location details.

Follow the prompts below to set up Screen time for your kid or family member;

1. Launch the Apple Watch app on your iPhone that was used to manage Watch for them.

2. Click on "All Watches," and then click on the watch under Family Watches.

3. Select "Done," click on "Screen Time," and then choose "Edit Screen Time Settings."

4. Click on settings like Downtime and Content & Privacy Restrictions in order to edit them.

On the same screen, you can as well access the Screen Time activity report for that family member's watch.

Alternatively, launch the Settings app on your own iPhone, click on "Screen Time," choose your kid's or family member's name under the Family heading and then choose a setting.

CHAPTER TWO

How to open apps on your Apple Watch

Get quick and easy access to apps on Watch from the Home Screen. The Dock even gives fast access to apps you deployed most often. You will be able to add about ten apps to your Dock so that you can have fast access to them.

How to show your apps on a grid or in a list

You can choose how you want apps to appear on your Watch's Home Screen. Apps can either be shown in list view or grid view. To select how you want your apps to appear on the Home Screen, follow the steps below;

1. Launch the Settings app on the Apple Watch.

2. Click o n "App View," and then select "Grid View" or "List View."

You can as well open Apple Watch app on your iPhone, click on "My Watch," select "App View," and then choose List View or Grid View.

How to open apps from the Home Screen

The way you open apps is a function of which you view you selected in the previous step above;

- *Using Grid view:* Click on the app icon. But If you are already present at the Home Screen, simply turn the Digital Crown to launch the app that is currently in the center of the Watch's display.

- *List view:* Rotate the Digital Crown and then click on an app.

You can go back to your Home Screen from any app by pressing your Watch's digital just once. Presses the Digital Crown again to switch to your Watch's Face (or if you are in grid view, click on ⌚ on your Home Screen).

If you wish to visit the last app that you used even when you are currently using another app, click twice on the Digital Crown.

How to open an app from the Dock

1. Press your side button and then rotate your Digital Crown to move through your apps in the Dock.

2. Click on an app to launch it.

How to choose which apps appear in the Dock

You can decide to display the apps you used recently in your Dock or even show up to ten of your favorite apps.

- *See recently used apps:* Launch the Watch app on your iPhone, click on "My Watch," select "Dock," and then choose "Recents." The most recently used app will show right at the top of your Dock while other apps will be positioned below just in the same order you last opened them.

- *See your favorite apps:* Launch the Watch app on your iPhone, click on "My Watch," select "Dock." Click on "Favorites," select "Edit," and then click on ⊕ beside the apps that you want to add. Drag the slider ☰ if you want to adjust the apps' order.

  When you select Favorites, the apps that you used most recently will be shown at the top of your Dock which gives you access to reopen such app very quickly. You can add the app to your Dock by clicking on "Keep in Dock."

- *Remove an app from your Dock:* Click the side button and then swiftly rotate the Watch's Digital Crown to the app that you plan to remove. Swipe left on that app and choose X.

- *Switch from your Dock to the Home Screen:* Move by scrolling to the bottom of your Dock and then click on "All Apps."

Tip: You can equally add apps that you use most as complications to watch face.

How to rearrange your apps in grid view

1. Navigate to your Watch's Home Screen by clicking the Watch's Digital Crown. If your Watch's screen is already in list view, launch the Settings app on your Watch, click on "App View," and then select "Grid View."

2. You can drag an app to a new place by pressing the Watch Digital Crown and then touch and hold on an app until it begins to jiggles.

3. Press the Watch's Digital Crown when you finished rearranging.

Or launch your Apple Watch app on the iPhone, select "My Watch," select "App View," and then click on "Arrangement." Touch and app icon, hold the icon for about five (5) seconds and then drag the app to another location on the Home Screen. When you are in the list view, you will see your apps arranged in an alphabetical order.

How to Remove an app from Apple Watch

- *Grid view:* On the Watch's Home Screen, touch and hold on any app icon until there is an X on the app icon, then click on the X to delete the app from your Watch. You should understand that any app you removed from your Apple Watch will still be available on your paired iPhone until you delete if from there equally.

- *List view:* Swipe your app to the left of the screen, then select 🗑 to delete it from your Watch. You should understand that any app you removed from your Apple Watch in list view will still be available on your paired iPhone until you delete if from there equally.

How to adjust app settings

1. Launch the Apple Watch app on iPhone.
2. Click on "My Watch," and then move down to view the apps that you have installed.
3. Select an app to change settings for the app.

When you set restrictions on iPhone from Settings > Screen Time > Content & Privacy Restrictions, the restriction also applies for your Watch. For instance, if you disable iPhone Camera on your iPhone, the Camera icon will also be removed from your Apple Watch Home Screen.

How to check storage used by apps

1. Launch the Settings app on the Watch.

2. Scroll to General and tap on "Usage."

Or launch your Apple Watch app from the iPhone, click on "My Watch," and then scroll to General > Usage.

How to tell time on Apple Watch

- *Raise your wrist:* The time shows on your watch face and in the clock when you are in grid view, and also in the top-right corner of some apps.

- *Hear the time:* Launch the Settings app on the Apple Watch, click on "Clock," and then turn on the "Speak Time." Hold any of your two fingers (whether left or right) on the face of your Watch to listen to the time. Your Watch can as well play chimes on the hour. From the Settings app on your Apple Watch, click on "Clock," and then turn on Chimes. Click on "Sounds" to choose between Bells or Birds.

- *Feel the time:* You can feel the time by tapping out on the wrist (that contains the Watch) when the Apple Watch is in a silent mode, launch the Settings app on the Watch, select "Clock," choose "Taptic Time," turn on the "Taptic Time," and then select an option.

Note: If you have previously disabled Taptic Time, your Apple Watch might be set to always speak the time. If you still want to use Taptic Time, you should first navigate to Settings, click on "Clock," and then turn on the "Control With Silent Mode" feature under Speak Time.

- *Ask Siri:* You will be able to ask Siri the time by raising your wrist and then say "What time is it?"

How to add an alarm on your Apple Watch

Use your Alarms app on the Apple Watch to play some certain sounds or to let your Watch vibrate at a set time.

Use Siri to add an Alarm. Ask something like: "Set alarm for 5 a.m."

How to set an alarm on Apple Watch

1. Launch the Alarms app on your Watch.
2. Click on "Add Alarm."
3. Click on "AM or PM," and then tap on the minutes or hours. You don't necessarily need to do this if you are using 24-hour time.

4. Rotate the Watch's Digital Crown to adjust the time and then click on "Set."

5. You can turn on or turn off the alarm by tapping the alarm switch. Or click on the alarm time to choose label, repeat and snooze options.
Tip: If you are thinking of creating an alarm that will tap your wrist but won't necessarily make a sound, simply turn on the silent mode.

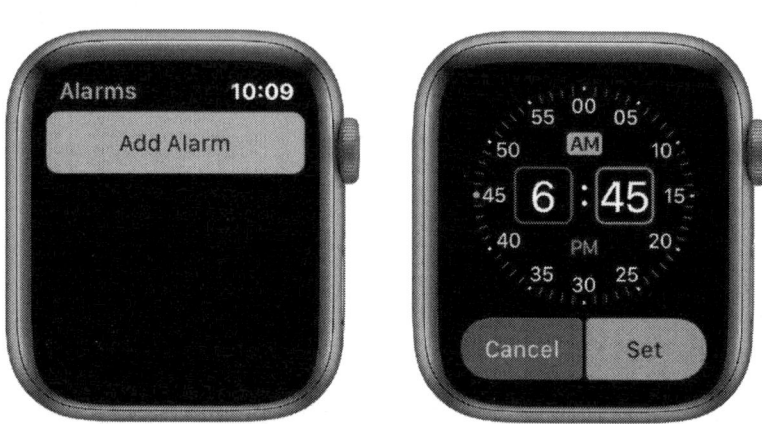

Don't let your alarm snooze

When your alarm makes a sound, you can choose Snooze to wait for several minutes before making another sound. If you want to disable snooze, you can follow the procedure below;

1. Launch the Alarms app on your Watch.

2. Choose the alarm that you want to disable Snooze for on your list of alarms and then toggle off the "Snooze" switch.

How to delete an alarm

1. Launch the Alarms app on your Watch.

2. Choose the alarm that you want to delete from the list of alarms.

3. Move to the bottom and then select "Delete."

How to skip a wake-up alarm

If you are tired for the day after some long strenuous activities, you can skip an alarm for that day by following the prompts below;

1. Launch the Alarms app 🕰 on your Watch

2. Click on the alarm that shows under Sleep | Wake Up and then choose "Skip for Tonight."

How to see the same alarms on both your iPhone and Apple Watch

1. Begin by setting an alarm on your iPhone.

2. Launch your Apple Watch app on the iPhone.

3. Click on "My Watch," select "Clock," and then turn on the "Push Alerts from iPhone" feature.

Your Watch will alert you when a particular alarm goes off so that you can either Snooze the alarm or dismiss the alarm. You won't be notified on the iPhone when your Watch alarm goes off.

How to set up Apple Watch as a nightstand clock with alarm

1. Launch the Settings app on the Apple Watch.
2. Scroll to General, tap on Nightstand Mode and then turn on the "Nightstand Mode" feature.

When the Nightstand mode is active and you connect your Watch's charger, you will see charging status, the active date and time and the actual time for any alarm you set. To view the time, click on the display or nudge the Apple Watch lightly.

If you plan your alarm with the Alarms app, the Apple Watch in the nightstand mode will wake you gently using a beautiful alarm sound.

When your alarm sounds, tap the Watch's side button to turn off the alarm, or click on the Digital Crown to snooze the alarm for about 8 to 9 minutes.

How to set a timer on Apple Watch

The Timer app on your Apple Watch will help you to keep track of your time. You can set the timers for 24 hours.

Ask Siri to set a timer. Prompt Siri with something like: "Set a timer for 40 minutes."

How to quickly set a timer

1. Launch the Timer app on the Apple Watch.
2. Select timer duration to initiate the timer.
3. Move down to select a custom time or recent time.

When your timer goes off, click on "Repeat" to begin a timer of the exact same duration.

How to create a custom timer

1. Launch the Timer app on the Apple Watch.

2. Move down to select a custom time.

3. Click on hours, seconds or minute and then rotate the Watch's Digital Crown to adjust.

4. Click on "Start."

Your Apple Watch will bring the last custom times under Recents.

How to open a stopwatch

Launch the Stopwatch app on Watch, or select the stopwatch on the face of your watch (if you have previously added Stopwatch or you are deploying the Chronograph or the Chronograph Pro watch face).

How to start, stop, and reset your stopwatch

Launch your Stopwatch app on Apple Watch and then carry out any of the settings below;

- *Start:* Click on the green Start button.

- *Record a lap:* Click on the white Lap button.

- *Record the final time:* Click on the red Stop button.

- *Reset the stopwatch:* Click on Lap button or the white Reset button.

The timing will still continue even if you go back to your watch face or launch other apps.

You can review and see results on the display you deployed for timing, or modify displays to analyze the lap times and your fastest/slowest laps (marked with green and red) in the exact format that you prefer.

Start or stop the stopwatch.

Record lap times.

How to change the stopwatch format

1. Launch your Stopwatch app on Apple Watch.

2. Click on the display to cycle through Analog, Digital, Graph and the Hybrid formats.

CHAPTER THREE

How to use Control Center on your Apple Watch

The Control Center on the Apple Watch give users an easy means to check battery, silence their watch, activate the "Do Not Disturb," turn their Watch into a flashlight, enable Airplane mode for Watch, activate the Theater mode and lots more.

How to open or close Control Center

- *Open Control Center:* From your watch face, simply swipe up. From any other screens, touch and then hold the bottom of your screen, then swipe up on the screen.

  Note: You won't be able to launch Control Center from Home Screen on the Apple Watch. Instead, press the Watch's Digital Crown to see the watch face or launch an app and then open the Control Center.

- *Close Control Center:* Swipe down from the top of your screen, or click on the Digital Crown.

How to rearrange Control Center

You will be able to rearrange the buttons in the Control Center by following the steps below;

1. Touch and then hold the bottom part of your screen, then swipe up on the screen to launch Control Center.

2. Navigate to the bottom of your Control Center and then tap "Edit."

3. Drag any button you want to rearrange to a new location.

4. Select "Done" when you are finished.

How to remove Control Center buttons

You will be able to remove any of the buttons in the Control Center by using these steps:

1. Touch and then hold the bottom part of your screen, swipe up on the screen to launch the Control Center.

2. Navigate to the bottom of your Control Center and then tap "Edit."

3. Click on the ⊖ located in the corner of the specific button that you wish to remove.

4. Select Done when you are finished.

To bring back any button that you have removed, launch the Control Center, select "Edit," and then click ⊕ located in the corner of the specific button that you want to restore. Click on "Done" when you are finished.

How to turn on the airplane mode on Watch

While flying with airlines, you might be allowed to go in with your Apple Watch and iPhone so far you have put them on Airplane mode. By turning on the Airplane mode, you have automatically turned off cellular connection, Bluetooth and Wi-Fi.

- *Turn on airplane mode on Apple Watch:* Simply touch the bottom of the Watch's screen and then hold, swipe up from the lower end of the screen to launch the Control Center and then select ✈ .

Ask Siri to turn on Airplane mode. Prompt Siri with anything like: "Turn on the airplane mode."

- *Place both the Apple Watch and your iPhone in airplane mode using one step:* Launch the Watch app from your iPhone, click on "My Watch," scroll to General, tap on Airplane Mode and then enable Mirror iPhone. When the iPhone and your Apple Watch are within acceptable Bluetooth range from each other (say 10 meters), the Airplane mode on one device is automatically enabled when you turn the Airplane mode on the other one.

When you have enabled the airplane mode, you will see ✈ from the top of your screen.

Note: Even when you turn on the Mirror iPhone, you will still have to disable Airplane mode separately on the Watch and on your iPhone.

How to use the flashlight on Apple Watch

You can use Watch's flashlight to notify others when you are going out - say for an evening workout - light nearby object so you can see clearly or light a darkened door lock.

- *Turn on the flashlight:* Simply touch the bottom of the Watch's screen and then hold, swipe up from the bottom area to launch the Control

Center and then select 🔦. Swipe to the left of the screen to select a mode—steady red light, steady white light or flashing white light.

- *Turn off the flashlight:* Click the Digital Crown or the side button, or swipe down from the top part of your watch face.

Use theater mode on Apple Watch

The Theater mode will restrict your Apple Watch display from automatically turning on raising your wrist, so the screen light is not coming up (just like Dark Mode). The Theater mode will also enable the silent mode and make the Walkie-Talkie status to be unavailable, although you will still be able to receive haptic notifications.

Simply touch the bottom of the Watch's screen and then hold, swipe up from the bottom to launch the Control Center and then select 🎭 and then click on "Theater Mode."

When the theater mode on your Watch is on, you will see 🎭 at the top of your Watch's screen.

You can wake your Apple Watch when your theater mode is on, click on the Watch's display, click on the Digital Crown or the side button, or rotate the Digital Crown.

Disconnect Apple Watch from Wi-Fi

You can as well disconnect temporarily from your Wi-Fi network and on models of Apple Watch with cellular, and rather deploy an available cellular connection – all from the Control Center.

Simply touch the bottom of the Watch's screen and then hold, swipe up from the bottom to launch the Control Center and then select 🛜 .

Your Apple Watch will disconnect temporarily from your Wi-Fi network. If you have set up cellular connection on your Apple Watch, the cellular connection will be activated if you have internet coverage. The Wi-Fi you connected to at any place is automatically remembered by your Apple Watch so that it can join the network automatically.

How to turn on silent mode

Simply touch the bottom of the Watch's screen and then hold, swipe up from the bottom to launch the Control Center and then select 🔔.

Note: If your Watch is charging, your alarms and timers will still make a sound even when you have put Watch in silent mode.

You can also launch the Watch app on your iPhone, click on "My Watch," select Sounds & Haptics and then enable the silent mode.

Tip: When you receive a notification, you can rest the palm of your hand on your Watch display (for about three seconds) to quickly mute the Apple Watch. You will sense a light tap which will allow you to know that the mute is on. Ensure you turn on Cover to Mute on the Apple Watch app on your iPhone—from settings, click on "My Watch" and then scroll to Sounds & Haptics.

How to turn on Do Not Disturb

Restrict your alarms and calls from lighting up your screen or making some sounds by using the "Do Not Disturb" feature. The Alarm and your heart rate notification will still be making sound nonetheless.

You will be able to turn on the "Do Not Disturb" for a set amount of time, until you move away from your current location, or until a particular calendar event ends. Simply touch the bottom of the Watch's screen and then hold, swipe up from the bottom to launch the Control Center and then select ☾. Choose from a list of options; On for 1 hour, On, On until I leave, On until the event ends or On until this evening.

You can also launch the Settings app ⚙ from the Apple Watch, click on "Do Not Disturb," and then turn on the "Do Not Disturb" feature.

You can automatically turn on the "Do Not Disturb" automatically when you want to begin a workout session by launching the "Settings app ⚙" on the Watch, click on "Do Not Disturb," and then turn on the "Workout Do Not Disturb" feature. You can as well launch the Apple Watch app from your iPhone by scrolling to "General," select "Do Not Disturb," and then turn on the "Workout Do Not Disturb" feature.

When the "Do Not Disturb" is enabled, you will see a crescent shaped icon 🌙 at the top of your screen.

Tip: To keep both the Watch and the iPhone silenced, launch the Apple Watch app on iPhone, click on "My Watch," scroll to General, select "Do Not Disturb" and then activate the "Mirror iPhone." So, whenever you enabled the "Do Not Disturb" on Apple Watch, it is also activated on your iPhone.

How to turn sleep mode on or off

Sleep mode brings a simple watch face with not so many apps and features and also helps you to turn on the Do Not Disturb. Ordinarily, the sleep mode will turn on and off automatically according to the sleep schedule you have created on your Watch, but you will be able to control this setting in the Control Center. Simply touch the bottom of the Watch's screen and then hold, swipe up from the bottom to launch the Control Center and then select 🛏. You can also exit the sleeping mode temporarily by turning/rotating your Watch's Digital Crown to unlock.

How to locate your iPhone with your Apple Watch

You can use your Apple Watch to locate your missing iPhone if it is within range.

Touch the bottom of the Watch's screen and then hold, swipe up from the bottom to launch the Control Center and then select .

Your iPhone will make a tone so that you will be able to track it down.

Tip: If you are in the dark, simply touch and hold on the Ping iPhone button and your iPhone will flashes as well.

If the iPhone is not in range of your Watch, you can try using the "Find My" from www.iCloud.com.

How to find your lost Apple Watch

If you misplace your watch, you can use the "Find My" to search for it.

1. From your iPhone, launch the "Find My" app.

2. Click on "Devices," and then choose your watch from the list.

You will be able to play a sound on the Apple watch, mark the Watch as lost, erase contents on your Watch and use Directions to access directions to it in the Maps.

In case of missing or stolen Apple Watch, you will be able to track your Watch using iCloud and Find My.

Adjusting screen brightness, haptics, sounds, and text size on your Watch 6 and Watch SE.

How to adjust brightness and text on Watch

Launch the Settings app ⚙ from the Watch and then choose "Display & Brightness" to make adjustment to the following settings;

- *Brightness:* Adjust the screen brightness by tapping on the Brightness controls or tap on the brightness slider and then turn your Digital Crown.

- *Text size:* Select "Text Size," and then click on the letters or rotate the Watch' Digital Crown.

- *Bold text:* Enable "Bold Text."

You can as well use your iPhone to carry out these settings. Launch the Apple Watch app on your phone, click on "My Watch," select "Display & Brightness" and then adjust texts and brightness.

How to Adjust Watch sound

1. Launch the Settings app from the Apple Watch.

2. Click on "Sounds & Haptics."

3. Click on the volume controls located under Alert Volume or select the volume slider and then turn Watch's Digital Crown to adjust volume.

You can also adjust Watch sound on your iPhone, launch the Watch app on your phone, select "Sounds & Haptics," and then drag the Watch's Alert Volume slider.

You will also be able to reduce loud sounds from headphones that you have connected to Watch. From the Sounds & Haptics setting on Watch, select "Reduce Loud Sounds," and then turn on the "Reduce Loud Sounds."

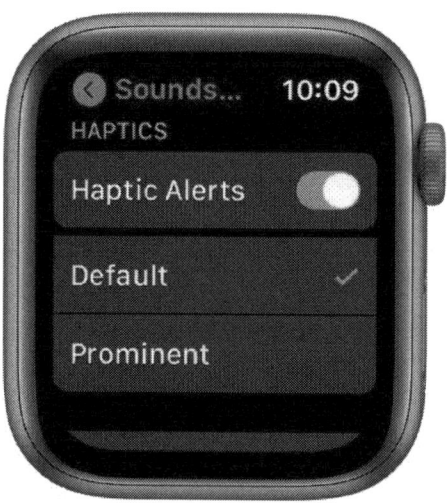

How to adjust haptic intensity

You will be able adjust the intensity of the wrist taps or haptics that your Watch uses for alerts and notifications.

1. Launch the Settings app from the Watch.

2. Click on "Sounds & Haptics," and then enable "Haptic Alerts."

3. Select between Prominent or Default.

You can as well adjust Haptics on your iPhone, launch the Watch app on your phone, select "Sounds & Haptics," and then select between Prominent or Default.

How to turn Digital Crown Haptics Off or On

On your Apple Watch SE and Watch 6, you sense clicks anytime you turn your Watch's Digital Crown to scroll. You can turn on/off this haptics by;

1. Launch the Settings app on the Watch.
2. Click on "Sounds & Haptics," and then turn on/off Crown Haptics.

You can also adjust turn on/off Digital Crown haptics on your iPhone, launch the Watch app on your phone, select "Sounds & Haptics," and then turn on/off Crown Haptics.

How to view and respond to notifications on Watch

Notifications such as messages, noise alerts, activity reminder, meeting invites etc are usually sent to your screen to get you informed about an upcoming event or keep you updated just about anything. Once a notification enters your Watch, your Watch brings it on immediately. But if you don't read the notification as it arrives, it will be saved on the Watch so that you can get to read it at a later time.

How to quickly respond to notification as they arrive

1. Raise your wrist to see any notification once you hear the sound or feel it.

2. You can navigate to the bottom part of the notification by turning the Watch's Digital Crown. You can as well open the corresponding app (that brought the notification) by tapping on the app icon.

3. Swipe down on a particular notification to dismiss such notification. Alternatively, you can move down to the bottom section of the notification and select "Dismiss."

How to see notifications you are yet to attend to

Any notification that you cannot respond as it enters will be saved in the Notification Center so that you can respond to it later. When you see a red dot at the top of the Watch's Screen, it means there is a notification that you are yet to read. To view such notification, use the steps below;

1. Open Watch's Notification center by swiping down on the Watch face. From some other screens on the Watch, touch and then hold the top of your screen and then swipe down. You will not be able to launch access the Notification Center while viewing your Home Screen on the Watch. But you can press the Watch's Digital Crown to scroll to your watch face, or launch an app and then access the Notification center.

2. Scroll through the list of your notification by scrolling up or down or turning the Watch's Digital Crown.

3. Select any notification from the list to view or respond to it.

To remove a notification from the Notification Center without necessarily reading it, swipe such notification to the left, and then click on X. You will be able to dismiss all notifications by going to the top of your screen and then choose "Clear all."

Tip: The small red dot that usually shows on the Watch face anytime you receive a notification is a notification indicator. You can disable the red dot by going to the settings app ⚙ on the Watch, click on Notifications and then turn the notification indicator off.

Choose how your notifications are delivered

By default, the same notification settings for your apps on the Watch are applicable and about the same thing as that on your iPhone. Nonetheless, you can still customize how most of your apps on the Watch display notifications. To do this, follow the steps below;

1. Launch the Watch app on your iPhone.

2. Click on "My Watch," and then select "Notifications."

3. Select the app (for instance, Messages app), choose Custom and then select an option. The available options are;

    - *Allow Notifications:* Select this to allow this app brings notification in the Notification center.

    - *Send to Notification Center:* Select this so that any notification coming to the Watch will be send straight to your Notification Center without notifying you through sound or showing notification.

    The following Apps support direct delivery to the Notification Center; Activity app, Calendar, Breathe, Messages app, Mail, Reminders, Wallet and Walkie-Talkie.

- *Notifications Off:* Choose this if you don't want the app to send notification.

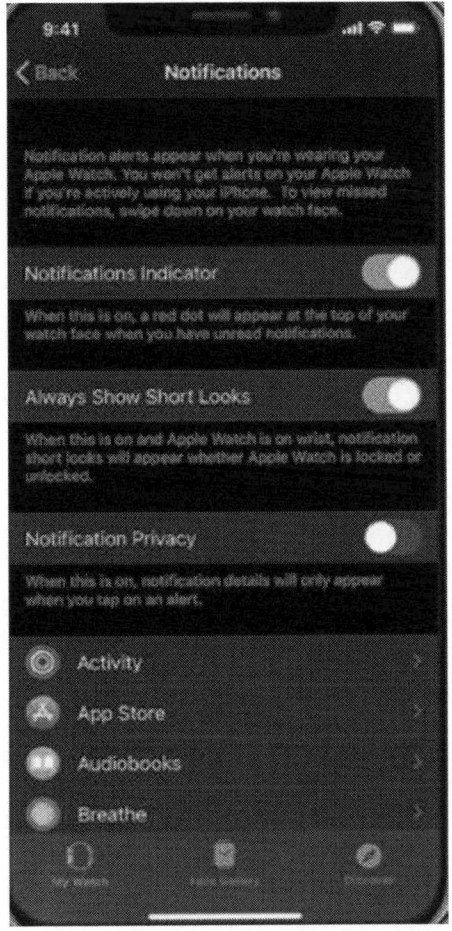

Your notifications preferences cab also be managed directly from your Watch when you swipe left on a notification and then tap ●●●. The following options may be applicable;

- *Deliver Quietly:* Select this so that any notification coming to the Watch will be send straight to your Notification Center without notifying you through sound or showing notification. If you want activate and hear apps notification alerts again, simply swipe left on any notification, click on ••• and then select "Deliver Prominently."

- *Turn Off on Apple Watch:* Choose this if you don't want the app to send notification.

How to use notification grouping

For each of the app on your Watch that enables notifications, you will be able to choose how your notifications will be grouped.

1. Launch the Watch app on iPhone.

2. Click on "My Watch," and then select "Notifications."

3. Select an app, click on Custom and then click on "Notification Grouping." The options here can include;

   - *Off:* Notifications will not be grouped.

   - *Automatically:* Watch uses info from the app to initiate separate groups. For instance, your News notifications will usually be grouped by the various channels that you follow—Aljazeera, CNN, People, Washington Post etc.

   - *By App:* Group all apps' notification.

How to silence all notifications on your Watch

Touch and then hold the bottom area of your screen, swipe up on the screen to launch the Control Center and then click on 🔔.

You will still be feeling a tap when a notification comes. To completely restrict sound *and* taps, touch and then hold the bottom area of your screen, swipe up on the screen to launch the Control Center and then click on 🌙.

Tip: When you receive a notification, you can rest the palm of your hand on your Watch display (for about three seconds) to quickly mute the Apple Watch. You will sense a light tap which will allow you to know that the mute is on. Ensure you turn on Cover to Mute on the Apple Watch app on your iPhone—from settings, click on "My Watch" and then scroll to Sounds & Haptics.

How to turn off short look notifications on your Apple Watch is locked

Whether you lock or unlock your Watch, the Watch – by default – will always bring short look notifications; which is a single screen that will display the name and icon of the app where the notification came from together with the title of the notification. You can decide to disable the short look notification when your Watch is locked.

1. Launch the Settings app from your Apple Watch.
2. Click on "Notifications," and then disable the "Always Show Short Looks."

How to keep notifications on your Apple Watch private

A quick summary follow by full details is displayed shortly anytime you raise your wrist to check a notification. For instance, when you receive a message alert, you will first see who sent it, and then the message will be prompted. You can disable the full notification from showing until you click on it. To do this, follow the steps below;

- Launch the Settings app from your Apple Watch.
- Click on "Notifications," and then enable "Notification Privacy."

How to use shortcuts on Apple Watch

The Shortcuts app on your Watch allows you to trigger any task with a mere tap. Get quick direction, create your favorite playlist and lots more by using the shortcut app. You can use shortcut from the shortcut app or add shortcut as complication to Watch face. Note that it is not all the shortcuts on your iPhone that are compatible with the Watch.

How to run a shortcut

1. Launch the Shortcuts app from the Apple Watch.
2. Select a shortcut.

How to add a shortcut complication on your watch

1. Touch the Watch face and hold on it, then click on "Edit."
2. Swipe left on the screen to get to the Complications screen and then select a complication.
3. Navigate to Shortcuts and then select a shortcut.

How to add more shortcuts to Apple Watch

1. Launch the Shortcuts app from your phone.

2. Click on ••• located in the top-right corner of the shortcut you selected.

3. Select ••• on your shortcut screen and then toggle on the "Show on Apple Watch."

Creating an emergency Medical ID with Watch

In case of emergency, a medical ID gives quick and short details about your health so that anyone attending to your or that want to rescue you can always have a brief idea of your health profile. The Apple Watch can be deployed to show this information. If you have a particular allergy, it is always good to document it in the Watch's emergency medical ID. If you are an adult - say 50 years and above - you should have an emergency medical ID that will include your exact date of birth. Your Apple Watch 6 and SE has a fall detection feature that is turned on by default if you are an adult above 55 years (can as well be turned on if you are above 18 years).

How to set up Medical ID on Watch

1. Launch the Health app on your phone.

2. Gently tap on your profile picture located at the upper right side and then tap on "Medical ID."

3. Select "Get started," and then input your information.

How to view your Medical ID on Apple Watch

1. On your Watch, hold the Watch's side button till you see the sliders.

2. Once the Medical ID slider shows up, drag it to the right.

If you cannot see the Medical ID on holding the Watch's side button, simply launch the Watch app on your iPhone, click on "My Watch," select "Health," chose "Medical ID," click on "Edit" and then toggle on the "show when locked" switch. You can hide the Medical ID when your Watch is locked by toggling off the "Show when locked" switch.

Tip: You can add emergency contacts to the Medical ID so that your Watch will alert your emergency contacts when it sends an emergency SOS call to the emergency services.

Recording an electrocardiogram with your ECG app on Apple Watch

The Apple Watch 6 and SE feature an electrical heart rate sensor which, together with your ECG app , enables users to record an ECG. The ECG need updated version of iOS (iOS 14 for instance) while the Watch series also need an updated WatchOS (Watch OS 7 for example). The ECG app doesn't work in all regions.

1. Launch the Health app on the Apple phone and then proceed to set up your ECG by following the onscreen guides.

    If you do not get a prompt to set up, click on "Browse" at the bottom right, choose "Heart," and then choose Electrocardiogram (ECG).

2. Launch the ECG app on the Watch.

3. Rest any of your arms on your lap on a table.

4. With your hand oppositely facing your watch, hold your finger on the Watch's Digital Crown and then wait a little bit while Watch records your ECG.

You don't necessarily have to click on the Watch's Digital Crown during the session.

Once the recording ends, you will see a classification. You can click on "Add Symptoms" and select your symptoms. Select "Save" if you plan to save the symptoms and then click on "Done." You can access the result on your iPhone by launching the Health app on the phone, select "Browse" located at the bottom right, click on "heart" and then tap on "Electrocardiograms (ECG)."

How to check heart rate on the Apple Watch

Heart rate gives you a measure of how well your body systems are functioning. Check the heart rate during walking, breathing, resting and any strenuous exercise.

See your heart rate

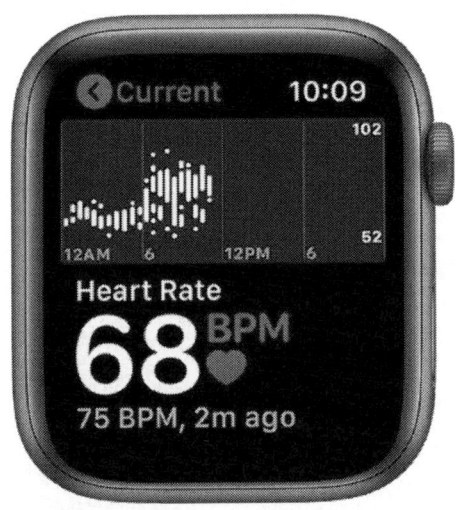

Launch the Watch's Heart Rate app on the Watch to see your current heart rate, resting rate and walking average rate.

As long as you continue wearing your Watch on your wrist, the Watch will keep measuring heart rate for you.

Check your heart rate during a workout

Your active heart rate, by default, will always show on your Multiple Metric workout view. Follow the guide below if you want to set which metric you want to see during a workout session.

1. Launch your Health app on iPhone.

2. Click on "My Watch," scroll to "Workout," tap "Workout View," and then choose a workout.

View a graph of your heart rate data

1. Launch the Health app on iPhone.

2. Click on "Browse" located at the bottom right side, click on "Heart," and then select "Heart Rate."

3. Swipe up and then click on "Add to Favorite" if you want to include heart rate in your summary.

You will be allowed to view your heart rate for the last day, week, month, year or even hours. Click on "Show More Heart Rate Data" and you will be able to check your heart rate range for the chosen periods. You can also view your; workout, walking average, breathe rate, resting and any low or high heart rate notification.

How to turn on your heart rate data

By default, the Apple Watch is monitoring your heart rate during; your workout session, for the heart rate app and Breathe sessions. If you have previously turned off the heart rate data; either by mistake or for any other reasons, you can turn it on again buy following the step below;

1. On the Apple Watch, launch the Settings app ⚙.

2. Navigate to Privacy and click on "Health."

3. Click on "Heart Rate," and then turn it on.

You can as well use the Watch app on your iPhone, click on "My Watch," select "Privacy" and then activate the heart rate by turning it on.

Let Apple Watch control your home.

You can automate your HomeKit-enabled accessories, like lights, smart plugs, window shades, thermostats, cameras, locks etc using your Watch. With Apple Watch, you can control anything in your home on your wrist.

The first time you launch Home app on the iPhone, the Apple setup assistant will help you to create a home. Then you can define the rooms, add your

HomeKit-enabled accessories, and also create scenes. Any accessory added as favorite on your iPhone will also be made available on the Watch.

Ask Siri. Prompt Siri with something like: "Turn off the lights in the kitchen."

Add a new accessory or scene to the Home app

Add a HomeKit-enabled accessory or create a scene by using the Home app on your iPhone. Any favorite accessory and scenes are also available on the Watch.

1. Click on "Rooms" from the iPhone's Home app to mark an item as favorite.

2. Swipe to the left or to the right to look for scene or the accessory and then touch and hold the accessory or scene.

3. Tap on the settings icon and then enable the "Include in Favorites."

Once you have successfully added a new scene or accessory to your favorite, it will show on the Apple Watch's Home app .

How to control smart home accessories and scenes

1. Launch your Home app on Watch.

2. Click on for an accessory and then adjust the settings.

3. Access more options by swiping to the left.

4. Click on "Done" to go back to the list of accessories.

You can control any scene by launching your Home app directly from the Apple Watch, and then select a scene to turn it off/on.

How to view a different home

In case you have set up more than one Home on your Watch, you will be able to select which Home you want to see on the Watch. Follow the steps below;

- Launch the Home app on Watch and then carry out one of the following:
    - If your Home Screen is showing, click on a home.
    - If the Home Accessories screen is displaying, click on < and then select a home.

How to access any of your Smart home accessories remotely with your Apple Watch

If you recently bought an Apple TV (probably the 3rd generation or later), and iPad (iPadOS 13 or iPadOS 14) that you left in your home, you will be able to access your HomeKit-enabled accessories right from your iPhone and the Apple Watch that you have paired with the iPhone. The Apple TV at home, the iPad and the HomePod serves like a home hub that allows you to communicate effectively with your home accessories even when you are nowhere near your home.

How to allow remote access

From your iPhone, scroll to Settings, select [*your name*], tap on iCloud and then turn on Home. You must be signed in with the same Apple ID on all of the devices you are using (iPhone or iPad).

Once you signed in with the same Apple ID and you have an Apple TV, pairing will take place automatically.

How to read mail in the Mail app

1. Launch the Mail app ✉ from your Apple Watch.

2. Turn/rotate the Watch's Digital Crown to explore the message list.

CHAPTER FOUR

SOME ESSENTIAL APPLE WATCH APPS

The Message App on Apple Watch

- Reading messages on your Apple Watch

You can read and manage any incoming message from your Watch, and also send a reply using Scrible, Dictate or preparing a custom response, or even switch to the iPhone to send a reply.

How to read a message on Apple Watch

1. When you sense a tap or hear a sound notifying you that you have a message, simply raise up your Watch to read it.

2. You can scroll to the bottom of your message by turning/rotating the Digital Crown.

3. Tap on the top part of your screen to quickly jump to the top of message. Tip: If there is a web link embedded within a message, you can click the link to see web-formatted contents that have been optimized for your Watch.

If you received the message not long ago, touch and then hold the top area of your screen, swipe down on your display to check the message notification and then tap on it. You can mark this message as read by scrolling down and then select "Dismiss." Likewise, you can dismiss the message notification without necessarily marking it message as read by pressing the Watch's Digital Crown.

Check when your messages were sent

Click on a conversation from your Messages ⭕ conversation list and then swipe left on any message from the conversation.

How to mute or remove a conversation

- *Mute a conversation:* On the Messages list, swipe left on the conversation and then choose 🌙.

- *Delete a conversation:* On the Messages list, swipe left on the conversation and then choose 🗑.

How to access photos, audio, and video in a message

Messages can have photos, videos and audio. Follow the procedures below to see and save them;

- *Photo:* Tap on the photo to see it, tap twice on the photo if you want the picture to fill the whole screen. Return to your conversation by tapping on the Back button< located in the top-left corner. If you plan to save this photo, launch the message in your iPhone's Messages app, and save it there.

- *Audio clip:* Click on the clip if you want to listen. The audio is usually deleted after 120 seconds to save space. But if you still want to save the audio, you can select "Keep" located below the audio clip. Doing this, the audio will be kept for 30 days and you can extend this on your iPhone: navigate to "Settings," tap on "Messages," scroll down to "Audio Messages," click on "Expire" and then choose "Never."

- *Video:* Click on a video inside a message if you want to play the video in full-screen. Click once to bring the playback controls. Tap twice on the video to zoom out the video and rotate/turn the Digital Crown if you want to adjust the video volume. Return to the conversation by tapping on the Back button.

You can save the video by opening the message in your message app on iPhone and then save the video there.

Choose how to be notified

1. Launch your Watch app on iPhone.

2. Click on "My Watch," and then select "Messages."

3. Select "Custom" if you plan to set the options for how you wish to be notified anytime you get a message.

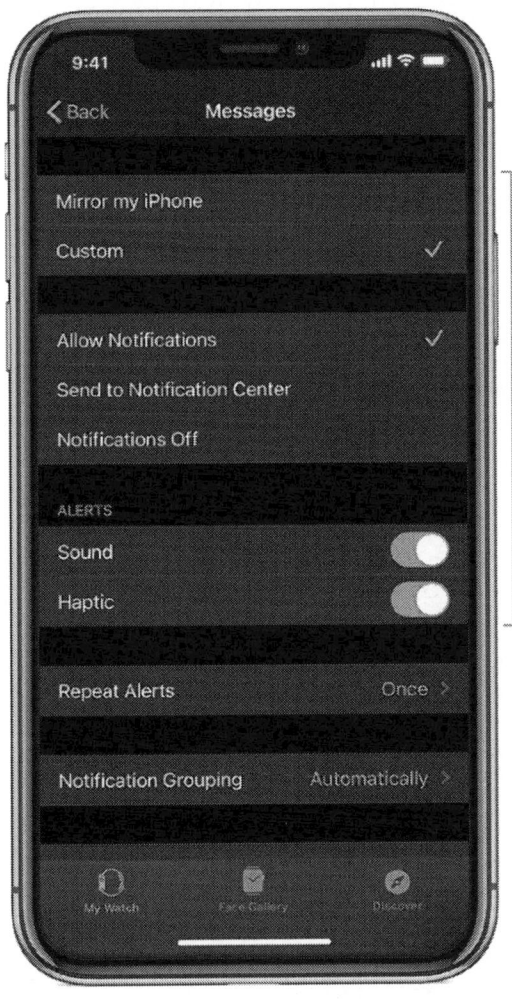

Set how you want to be notified.

Send messages from Apple Watch

Ask Siri. Prompt Siri with something like: "Ask David to see me in the office by 4PM." And then lower (bring down) your wrist to send it.

How to create a message on your Apple Watch

1. Launch the Messages app ⭕ on Watch.

2. Navigate to the top of your screen and then select "New Message."

3. Click on "Add Contact," choose a contact from your list of recent conversations that shows up and then select an option:

   - Click on 🎤 to search for anyone on your contacts list or to dictate a particular phone number.

   - Click on 👥 to select from your list of contacts.

   - Tap on ⌗ to input a phone number.

How to reply to a message

Turn/rotate Watch's Digital Crown to navigate to the bottom of your message and then decide how you want to reply.

To respond as fast as possible with a Tapback, tap twice on a specific message in a conversation and then select a Tapback. The Tapback is just like a thumb-up, an exclamation or a heart to give a job well done message or emphasize a point.

How to send a reply directly to one message in a conversation

When you are in a group conversation, you will be able to direct your response inline to a specific message from someone. This will help organize the conversation for easy tracking and understanding.

1. While you are in a Messages conversation, tap and hold on the message that you plan to reply to and then select Reply.

2. Input your response and then hit "Send."

The only person that will receive this message is the person to which the reply is intended for.

How to compose a message on your Apple Watch

Composing a message with Apple Watch can be done in a number of ways;

- *Send a smart reply:* Scroll down to view the list of handy phrases that you can use in your message—when you see one, simply tap on it to send.

    You can add your own phrase by opening the Watch app on your iPhone, click on "My Watch," scroll to Messages, tap on "Default Replies," and then select "Add Reply." You can customize your default replies by tapping on "Edit," and then drag each default reply to reorder them or click on ⊖ to delete any default reply.

    If the smart replies are not in the language you wish to use, scrolls down, click on Languages and then select a language. The available languages that you will see here are those languages that you have enabled on iPhone from Settings, select "General," tap on "Keyboard" and choose "Keyboards."

- *Dictate text:* Click on 🎤 , voice what you want to send and then choose "Done." You can voice punctuation, just like you speak texts—for instance, "did you get the message question mark." This will put question mark (?) after your message.

If you are using more than one language during texts (say English and Spanish) and you noticed that your dictation is not transcribed as it should (in the right language), you can decide to send the message as an audio clip. Or, better still change your dictation language by tapping on 🌐 located at the lower-left and then select a language.

- *Create an audio clip:* Launch Apple Watch app from your iPhone, click on "My Watch," scroll to Messages, select "Dictated Messages," and then click on Audio, Transcript or Audio or Transcript. If you choose Audio, the message recipient will receive your dictated message as an audio clip and will be able to listen to it, and rather not a text message that can be read. If you select Transcript or Audio, you will be able to select the format for the message when you send the message.

- *Scribble a message:* Tap on 👆, then input your message. While writing, kindly rotate your Watch's Digital Crown to view predictive text options and then choose one by tapping on it. Click on "Send" to send your message. Select a different language by tapping on 🌐 from the lower-left and then choose a language.

Note: Scribble is currently not compatible with all languages.

- *Send emoji:* Tap on 🙂, select a category and then scroll to access available images. When you see the right symbol, simply select it to send.

- *Send a Memoji sticker:* Click on 😀, click on an image from the Memoji Stickers collection and then select a variation to send it.

- *Send a sticker:* Click on 🐵, navigate to the bottom and then choose "More Stickers." Click on a sticker to send the sticker. You can create a new sticker or view all your stickers by deploying the Messages app on iPhone.

Use Apple Pay to send and receive money

1. Launch your Messages app 💬 on Apple Watch.

2. Initiate a new chat or proceed with an existing conversation.

3. Click on 💲.

4. Choose an amount that you want to send by using the Watch's Digital Crown and then select Pay.

5. Click twice on the Watch's side button to send.

Note: The Apple Cash menu might not work in all regions of the world. In fact, the Apple Cash is only working in the United States of America currently. The decision of whether Apple will extend this feature to other countries of the world is still unknown as at the time of writing this guide.

Share your location

You can send a map to someone detailing your active location by scrolling down and tapping on "Send Location."

On the iPhone you are using to pair with Watch, ensure that you have turned on the "Share My Location" feature by scrolling to Settings, tap on [*your name*], select "Find My" and choose "Share My Location." Alternatively, you can also get this done on your Apple Watch with cellular by launching the "settings app," scroll to "Privacy," select "Location Services" and then enable the "Share My Location."

How to contact the person you are messaging directly

1. Scroll down while you are currently viewing a conversation.

2. Click on "Details" and then choose ,   or .

THE MUSIC APP ON YOUR APPLE WATCH

Adding music to your Apple Watch

You can add good music to your Watch and listen to them wherever you found yourself. It doesn't matter whether you have your iPhone with your or not.

How to select which playlists should be added automatically to the Apple Watch

If you subscribe to Apple Music, music you have listened to recently will be added automatically to Watch. If you are yet to listen to any music, music recommended from Apple Music will be added. To modify which playlists should be added automatically, follow the steps below;

1. Launch the Watch app from your iPhone.

2. Click on "My Watch," and then choose Music.

3. Turn on individual playlists.

How to add albums and playlists to your Apple Watch

4. Launch the Watch app from your iPhone.

5. Click on "My Watch," and then choose Music.

6. Select "Add Music" below Playlists & Albums.

7. Add albums and playlists to your Watch by selecting albums and playlists.

Tip: You can use your Music app on the iPhone to create some playlists for the music that you want to be listening to on your Watch—might be any music that encourages you during a training or workout session, for instance.

How to add a workout playlist to your Apple Watch

8. Launch the Watch app from your iPhone.

9. Click on "My Watch," and then choose "Workout."

10. Select Workout Playlist and then tap a playlist.

This playlist you have added will always play automatically whenever you begin a workout unless you are currently listening to some other audio or music.

View how much music has been stored on your Apple Watch

1. Launch the Settings app on the Apple Watch.

2. Scroll to General and tap on "Usage."

You can also access the Apple Watch app from your iPhone, click on "My Watch," scroll to General and then select "Usage."

How to remove music from your Apple Watch

1. Launch the Watch app from your iPhone.

2. Click on "My Watch," and then select Music.

3. You can disable any playlist (you don't want) that was automatically from your Watch.

4. To delete some other music that you have personally added to your Watch, select "Edit," and then click on ![minus] next beside the unwanted items.

Note: Any music you deleted from your Apple Watch will still remain on your iPhone.

How to play your music on Apple Watch

Utilize your Music app ![music icon] on Watch to select and play music on your Apple Watch. You will be able to play music saved on Apple Watch, monitor and control music on your iPhone, and also stream music from the Apple Music if you are a subscriber.

Use Siri. Prompt Siri with something like: "Play 'All around me' by Justin Bieber"

Play music for you

If you subscribe to Apple Music, you will be able to play music chosen just for you.

1. Launch your Music app ![music icon] from your Apple Watch.

2. Navigate to the top area of your Watch's screen; choose Listen Now to see a curated feed of your playlists and albums chosen based on your likes and dislikes.

3. Click on a category, select an album or a playlist and then click on ▶.

    If you click on a station, it will start playing in your Radio app on the Apple Watch.

The Phone App on Apple Watch

How to answer your call on Watch

When you sense or hear the notification for the incoming call, just raise your wrist to check who the caller is.

- *Send the call to your voicemail:* Click on the red button (Decline button) from your incoming call notification.

- *Answer calls directly from your Apple Watch:* Click on your Answer button to take the call using the Watch's in-built microphone and the speaker or any Bluetooth device that has been successfully with the Apple Watch.

- *Answer calls using your iPhone or rather send text message:* Tap on ••• and then choose any option that you want. If you choose "Answer on iPhone," your call will be placed on hold and your caller will continue to hear a repeated sound alert until you answer the call on the paired iPhone.

If you cannot find the iPhone, simply touch and then hold the lower end of the screen, swipe up, and then choose 📳 on the Apple Watch.

Things you can do while you are on a call

If you are currently attending to a call that is not using the FaceTime audio, you can switch the call to your iPhone, adjust the volume of the call, input additional digits or numbers with the keypad and switch your call to some other audio devices.

- *Switch the call from Apple Watch to an iPhone:* While you are on a call on the Apple Watch, unlock the iPhone and then click on the green bar or button you will see at the top of your screen.

  You can silence any incoming call by mere pressing the palm of your hand right on your watch display for about three seconds. Just ensure that you have turned on the "Cover to Mute"—launch the Settings app from your Watch, select "Sounds & Haptics" and then enable the "Cover to Mute."

- *Adjust the volume of the call:* Turn/rotate Watch's Digital Crown. Tap on the mute icon if you want to mute your own end of the call – if you are on a conference or group call for instance.

- *Input some additional digits during a call:* Click on tap on Keypad and then press the digits.

- *Switch your call to an audio device:* Click on ••• and then select a device.

When you are on a FaceTime Audio call, you will be able to adjust the call volume, choose the audio destination by tapping on ••• and mute the audio call by clicking on the mute icon.

Listening to voicemail on Watch

If a caller drops a voicemail for you – probably because he or she was unable to reach you on time with a phone call – you will receive the notification. Simply click on the "Play button" in that notification to hear the voicemail. If you want to hear the voicemail at a later time, launch the Phone app from your Apple Watch and then select Voicemail.

From your voicemail screen, you will be able to do any of these;

- Adjust the Voicemail volume with Digital Crown
- Start Playback and stop it.
- Skip forward or backward five seconds
- Call the person back
- Delete/remove the voicemail

How to make phone calls on Apple Watch

Ask Siri. Prompt Siri with statement like;

- "Call James"

- "Dial the number 333 222 5649"

- "Call David FaceTime audio"

How to make a call

1. Launch your Phone app on the Watch.

2. Select "Contacts," and then rotate/turn your Watch's Digital Crown. This allows you to scroll through your contacts list.

3. Select the contact that you plan to call and then tap on the phone button.

4. Tap FaceTime Audio to start a FaceTime audio call, or tap a phone number.

5. Adjust the volume (either reduce or increase) during your call by turning the Watch's Digital Crown.

Tip: If you want to send a call to someone that you have recently spoken with, just select "Recents" and then choose the person's contact. If you want to send a call to someone that you have marked as favorite on your iPhone, simply select Favorite and then choose the person's contact.

How to input a phone number on the Apple Watch

1. Launch your Phone app ![icon] on the Watch.

2. Tap on Keypad, input the number and then select ![icon].

You can as well input additional digits or numbers with your keypads while you are currently on a call. Simply click on ![icon] and then tap on your Keypad button.

How to send calls over Wi-Fi

In case the cellular carrier you used on your Watch supports Wi-Fi calling, you can deploy your Watch to send and receive calls over a Wi-Fi instead of using your cellular network. This is also possible even when the paired phone is not near you or you have turned it off. The only thing is that your Watch need to be within acceptable range of a Wi-Fi network that you have previously connected your Apple phone to. To do this, follow the steps below;

1. From your iPhone, navigate to Settings, select "Phone," click on "Wi-Fi Calling," and then enable both "Wi-Fi Calling on This iPhone" and the "Add Wi-Fi Calling For Other Devices."

2. Launch your Phone app 📞 from the Apple Watch.

3. Choose a contact and then click on 📞.

4. Choose the phone number of the person that you want to call or the FaceTime address of the one you want to call.

Note: You can send an emergency call over a Wi-Fi, but when possible, deploy your iPhone over a secured cellular connection instead—as the location detail is actually more accurate. Ensure that the emergency address is an updated emergency address detailing your current location and health profile. To do this, from your iPhone, navigate to Settings, select "Phone" click on "Wi-Fi Calling," and then select "Update Emergency Address." If the emergency services cannot locate you, they will go straight to your emergency address and it is very helpful.

How to choose a photo album and manage your storage on Apple Watch

The album on your iPhone shows photos of your choosing in the Photo app on the Apple Watch. Photos that you have synchronized on iPhone are stored in the Apple Watch. Upon first purchase of the Apple Watch, it is designed to show photos from only your favorite album (photos you have marked as favorite), although this can be changed as you will soon see.

How to choose the album you want to store on Apple Watch

1. Launch the Apple Watch application from your iPhone.

2. Click on "My Watch," scroll to Photos, click on "Selected Photo Album," and then select the album.

To remove/delete a photo permanently from your Watch, launch your Photos app on iPhone, then remove/delete the image from your synchronized album.

You can create a new album for your Apple Watch photos with the Photos app on iPhone.

How to limit photo storage on your Apple Watch

The amount of photos you will be able to save on your Watch is a function of the available space on your Watch. You might need to place a limit to the number of photos saved on Watch if you want to save some spaces for audios and some other contents or files.

1. Launch the Watch app from your iPhone.

2. Tap on "My Watch," scroll to Photos and select Photos Limit.

You will be able to access how many photos are saved on the Watch with any of the methods below;

- Launch the Settings app ⚙ from Apple Watch, then scroll to General and select "About."

- Launch the Settings app ⚙ from Apple Watch, click on "My Watch," then scroll to General and select "About."

To check how much space has been used to save your photos on Watch, navigate to General and tap on "Usage in the Apple Watch app."

How to take a screenshot of Apple Watch

1. Launch the Settings app ⚙ from Apple Watch, then scroll to General and then turn on the "Enable Screenshots" option

2. Simultaneously press the Watch's Digital Crown and its side button to take a picture of your Watch's screen.

The screenshots will be saved in Photos on the iPhone.

How to view your photos on the Apple Watch

The Photo app is where you can get to browse all your photos. The browsed photo will be displayed on the Watch's face.

How to quickly browse photos on your Apple Watch

Launch the Photos app from your Watch and carry out any of the actions below to quickly browse your photos;

- Tap on a photo with your finger to view the photo.

- Swipe right or left on the photos screen to view other photos.

- Turn your Watch's Digital Crown if you want to zoom any photo.

- Use two fingers together or use the thumb with a finger to zoom out on a photo. This kind of Zooming out will let you see the whole photo.

How to view a Live Photo on your Apple Watch

The Live Photo icon is always located at the bottom right side of any photo. Touch and then hold the photo to see it.

How to show a photo on the watch face

Tap on while you are viewing a photo in your Photos app on the Apple Watch, and then select "Photos" under the "Create Watch Face." You can as well create a Kaleidoscope –like watch faces based on the photo, or add another Photos watch face in your Watch app from your iPhone.

Tip: It is very easy to create a Watch face on iPhone running iOS 11 and latest iOS like the iOS 14. To do this, launch your Photos app from your iPhone, select a photo, click on , swipe up and then select "Create Watch Face."

How to view a photo memory on your Apple Watch

You can access photo memories—ranging from forgotten moments to favorite from the Photo library – on the Watch.

- *View a recent memory from your Siri watch face:* Select the Siri watch face and then select a memory.

- *View photos from Memories on the watch face:* Launch the Apple Watch app from your iPhone, select "Face Gallery," tap on the Photos watch face and then select "Dynamic."

The Dynamic watch face shows photos from your recent Memories and it is automatically updated as you have new memories.

CHAPTER FIVE

About Apple Watch Wallet

Any card or pass that you have successfully added to your Wallet app on iPhone can be easily accessed with the Wallet app on the Watch. The Cards and Passes that are supported are;

- *Cards for Apple Pay (this is not present in all regions):* Apple Cash, debit card, credit card, store card, prepaid card and transit card.
- *Passes: This includes movie tickets, reward cards,* boarding passes etc.

Using Apple Pay on the Apple Watch

Apple Pay brings a secured, easy and private way to make payments on the Apple Watch. When you have successfully stored your cards in your iPhone's Wallet app and also added the same card to your Apple Watch, you will b able to utilize Apple Pay in any of these ways;

- *In contactless apps and payments:* Deploy your debit card, credit card and prepaid cards that you have successfully added to your Wallet app to carry out purchases in any store that accepts contactless transaction and in all apps that work with Apple Pay.

Upon setting up Apple Pay in the Watch app on iPhone, you can now make purchases in stores, and it doesn't even matter whether you have your iPhone with you or not; your Watch is all that is needed. The Apple Pay is not, as of now, present in all regions of the world.

- *Person to person payments:* Starting from Watches running WatchOS 4 up to the latest Watch OS 7, it becomes especially very easy to request for and send your money securely right in Messages or by just prompting Siri.

- *Transit cards:* You can also add transit cards. The Transit cards are used to pay for transport across places and countries. You will see your Transit card at the top section of the collection in your Wallet app, just above your Passes. The banks that are Apple Pay Participatory banks are most top banks in the United States (like the American Bank (IA), 1st National Bank of Scotia etc), Brazil, Canada etc.

Note: You won't be able to use the Apple Pay service on your Watch once you unpaired it from the iPhone you are pairing it with or you turn off your Passcode. In fact, when you do these, any card you have added to your Wallet will be removed automatically. For users that have turned off their wrist detection, they will be required to input their passcode each time they use Apple Pay.

Setting up Apple Pay on your Apple Watch

How to add your card to Apple Watch

1. Launch your Apple Watch app from your iPhone.

2. Click on "My Watch," and then select "Wallet & Apple Pay."

3. If there are cards on your other Apple phones, bud or devices, or just cards that you have removed recently, select "Add" just next to the card that you wish to add and then input the CVV for the card.

4. For any other card, select "Add Card," and then proceed with the onscreen instructions.

Your card issuer may need extra steps in order to confirm your identity.

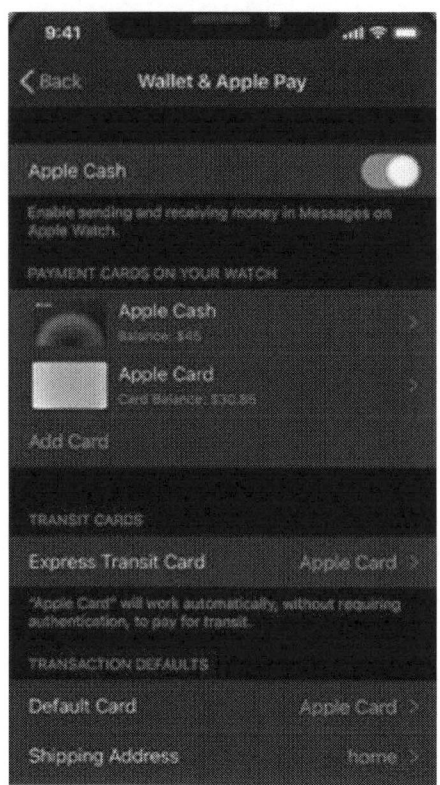

How to choose a default card

1. Launch your Watch app from your iPhone.

2. Click on "My Watch," select "Wallet & Apple Pay," click on "Default Card," and then choose the card.

Reorder payment cards

Launch your Wallet app from your Apple Watch, touch a card and hold on the card, then drag the card to a new place.

On Apple Watch that you set up for your child or family member (managed Apple Watch), you will be able to touch and then drag both the Passes and the payment card.

How to delete/remove a card from Apple Pay

1. Launch your Wallet app from your Apple Watch.

2. Tap to choose a card.

3. Move down and then choose Delete.

You can as well use the Apple Watch app from your iPhone, click on "My Watch," select "Wallet & Apple Pay," click on the card that you plan to remove and then click on "Remove This Card."

How to Find the Device Account Number for a card

When you send a payment using your Apple Watch, your Device Account Number of the card will be sent together with the payment to the merchant. You can see the last four (4) digits of the account number by following the steps below;

1. Launch your Wallet app from your Apple Watch.

2. Tap to choose a card and then click on "Card Information."

Note: If you choose an Apple Card, you will need to input your Apple Watch password before you will be allowed to access the details of the card.

You can as well use the Apple Watch app from your iPhone, click on "My Watch," select "Wallet & Apple Pay" and then choose the card.

How to change your default transaction details

If you want to change your transaction information – like your email, shipping address, phone number and default debit or credit card – follow the steps below;

1. Launch the Watch app from your iPhone.

2. Tap on "My Watch," click on "Wallet & Apple Pay," and then scroll down to view Transaction Defaults.

3. Select an item to edit the item.

What to do if your Apple Watch is stolen or lost

The following are steps that you can take if you have misplaced your Watch or it has been stolen;

- Try to put the Watch in lost mode to suspend any payment immediately.

- From your favorite web browser on your iPhone, navigate to appleid.apple.com and sign in with your Apple ID to disable yourself from paying with your debit card and credit card in Wallet. This is to prevent anyone from having unauthorized access to pay with your Wallet.

  In the Devices section, select the device and then tap the "Remove All" located under Apple Pay.

- Notify the cards issuers.

How to pay for a purchase in a store with Apple Watch

1. Double-click on the Watch's side button.
2. Scroll down to select a card.
3. Position the Apple Watch within a small centimeter of a contactless card reader and let the Watch display face the reader.

A light tap and beep will confirm that your payment information has been sent. You will get an alert on your Notification Center when your transaction has been confirmed.

Within your Apple Wallet, you will be able to turn off history and notifications for your individual cards. Simply launch your Apple Watch app on iPhone, click on "My Watch," scroll to "Wallet & Apple Pay," click on a card, select "Transactions," and then turn on/off the "Show History and Allow Notifications."

How to make a purchase within an app

1. When you making some purchases from an app on your Watch, select the Apple Pay option when you want to check out.

2. Review the billing details, payment and your shipping information and then double-click on the side button to make payment with the Apple Watch.

About the Author

 Newel Goman is a seasoned tech enthusiast with over 17 years of experience in the ICT industry. He has passionately followed and reviewed advancement in tech over the years. He enjoys figuring out how to simplify complex problems. Newel, holds a Bachelor and a Master's Degree in Computer Science and Information Communication Technology, respectively from Princeton University.

Manufactured by Amazon.ca
Bolton, ON